**Teacher-to-Teacher Series**

NEA Teacher-to-Teacher Books

Printing History
First Printing: March 1994

NOTE: The opinions expressed in this book should not be construed as representing the policy or position of the National Education Association. Materials published by the NEA Professional Library are intended to be discussion documents for educators who are concerned with specialized interests of the profession.

CREDITS: *Series Editor:* Mary Dalheim. *Contributing Editor:* Vincent Ercolano. *Production Coordinator:* Linda Brunson. *Art Design:* NoBul Graphics.

Library of Congress Cataloging-in-Publication Data
Innovative discipline.
     p. cm. — (Teacher-to-Teacher series)
   Includes bibliographical references.
   ISBN 0-8106-2904-6
     1. School discipline — United States. 2. School Psychology — United States.
I. NEA Professional Library (Association) II. Series.
LB3011.I55 1994
371.5'8 —dc20   [20]   94-5189
               CIP

Contents

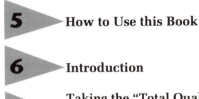

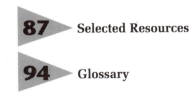

How to Use this Book

Innovative Discipline is no ordinary book. It is part of the NEA Professional Library's Teacher-to-Teacher Series in which classroom teachers speak directly to other teachers—like you—about their school restructuring efforts.

Printed in the upper right-hand corner of every book cover in the series is a routing slip that encourages you to pass the book on to colleagues once you have read it—in other words, to spread the word about school change.

Book topics cover areas such as large-scale school change, student assessment, cross-age grouping, and integrating students with special needs into regular classrooms.

Read the First-Person Stories

Inside each book you will find six or more stories from teachers across the country who discuss, step by step, how they tackled a specific restructuring challenge. They will describe what worked and didn't work, and provide you with any diagrams, checklists, or tables they think other teachers would find useful.

Write Your Own Ideas in the Book

At the end of each story in a book is an area called Reader Reflections. This area is for you and any colleague who reads the story to write related insights and action points for your school or school district to consider.

You see, the purpose of the Teacher-to-Teacher Series is not only to spread the word about school change but to encourage other teachers to participate in its exploration.

Discuss Your Thoughts With Colleagues

Once you have routed a book through your school, you can meet with colleagues who contributed to the Reader Reflections sections and expand upon your thoughts.

Go Online

Believe it or not, the communication and sharing doesn't have to stop there. If you would like to discuss a Teacher-to-Teacher Series topic with other teachers across the country, you can. Any NEA member who subscribes to the America Online electronic network can participate in an ongoing forum on these and other education topics.

The National Education Association's area on the network is called NEA Online. Once signed on to NEA Online, just keyword to *NEA Prof Library*.

To subscribe to NEA Online, call 1-800-827-6364, ext. 8544.

Introduction

Recent Gallup Polls and various education surveys indicate that student discipline remains number one on teachers' lists of troublesome concerns.

It seems only logical then that many educators who are active in the current school-change movement are experimenting with innovative ways to minimize student disruptions and maximize students' self-respect and respect for others. The six first-person stories in this book discuss some very different efforts in this arena.

Total Quality Management

Total Quality Management (TQM) is a concept most often associated with W. Edwards Deming and the business world. According to Deming, 80 to 90 percent of problems in an organization can be traced to systemic causes (i.e., rules, expectations, and traditions) over which individuals have little control. Therefore, he believes that when problems arise, management should look for causes in the system and work to remove them before casting blame on workers.

Teachers at Rawlings Elementary School in Pinellas County, Florida, decided to put this TQM premise to work in their classrooms. In the first chapter of this book, four Rawlings teachers tell how they use the Plan-Do-Study-Act Cycle of TQM to monitor and improve their management of student behavior.

Peer Mediators

At Orchards Elementary School in Lewiston, Idaho, teachers believe that conflict is a natural occurrence and that, in most cases, students are capable of finding their own peaceful solutions to conflicts that arise.

As a result, teachers introduce conflict resolution skills to all students, at all grade levels. They also select and train certain students (in grades four through six) to be conflict managers (CMs) on the playground. The CMs' task is to help other students find positive ways to resolve minor disagreements.

In the second story in this book, Orchards Elementary teachers Donna Johnson and Marcy Eisele discuss their faculty's efforts in conflict resolution and how these efforts have enriched the entire school community.

Student Court

At Lassiter Middle School in Louisville, Kentuck[y] seventh grade social stud[ies] teacher Fronda Yanc[e] became very frustrate[d] over the amount of clas[s]room time she spent dea[l]ing with petty distur[b]ances. She decided to es[t]ablish a student-operate[d] court system that woul[d] handle these minor prob[]lems outside of her in[]structional time.

In her story, Frond[a] tells how she designed [a] peer-operated court (calle[d] the Review Board) tha[t] basically emulates the American system o[f] justice.

The results? Teacher frustration and discipline problems have dropped dramatically, and student Review Board members (as well as case defendants) are experiencing important lessons in responsibility and the U.S. legal system.

Support Group

Twice a week at Tom Joy Elementary School in Nashville, Tennessee, sixth grade teacher Susan Adler conducts a support group meeting with her students to help them deal with pre-adolescent problems in positive, appropriate ways.

In her story, Susan describes how the meetings ensure emotional safety and confidentiality while at the same time they help students to develop important problem-solving skills, which, in turn, can help deter many potential discipline problems.

Mixed Bag

A few years ago, Chickasha Intermediate in Chickasha, Oklahoma, was a school with a "bad rep." It was known throughout the county as a school with severe discipline problems and plunging morale, until one day the staff got together and developed a package of discipline initiatives that turned this school into a happy, welcoming place to learn.

In their inspiring story, three Chickasha teachers and their principal share some of their most effective strategies. You'll find that these folks borrowed from a variety of discipline camps to come up with a formula that works for them. They discuss everything from reward systems to classroom rules to mastery learning to cooperative learning activities to parent shadowing.

Integrated Discipline

At the Independent Learning Center (ILC) in Woodland, California, at-risk high school students learn the art of self-discipline through a program that promotes individual responsibility, self-esteem, and most important, *integrated discipline.*

Integrated discipline is a process that meshes all school rules and expectations into the daily learning environment. In her story, school coordinator/teacher Sandi Redenbach describes exactly how teachers do this "meshing" at the ILC.

Final Impressions

The six stories in this book barely begin to cover the new work educators are doing in the area of discipline. Collectively, however, they reflect two predominant themes in discipline innovation.

First, that there is not just one "right way" to manage behavior. All of the teachers in this book have developed success-ful yet very different approaches.

Second, that discipline should be child-centered —that it should work toward developing self-control and personal commitment to rules and values. Teachers can do this by emphasizing student understanding of the general principles behind rules, by soliciting student input in setting these rules and complying to them, and by using mutual problem solving whenever possible.
—Mary Dalheim
Series Editor

Notes:

_____

_____

_____

_____

_____

_____

TAKING THE "TOTAL QUALITY" ROAD

When it came to choosing behavior management techniques, these Florida elementary teachers took the Total Quality Management road, and that's made all the difference!

1 Year after year, children come to school expecting to join a system that rewards compliance and provides clear-cut consequences for noncompliance. Faced with this traditional system, most students base their behavior almost entirely on a rigid structure of rewards and punishments.

The traditional system's teachers, accepting full responsibility for the good and bad behavior of their students, often end up acting more like police officers than educators. They spend 12 years teaching children how to follow rules and very little time teaching them how to make positive choices that will enable them to work with others.

The child who has never been taught to search for alternatives, or who has never been shown that there may even be more than one way to handle a problem, never grows under this system.

At Rawlings Elementary in Pinellas County, Florida, we believe that training our students to be responsible for their learning, and teaching them problem-solving strategies, will help to make them self-disciplined and inde-pendent. That, in turn, will increase our opportunities to do the job we were trained to do—teach.

We've developed a number of ways to provide this training, and in the following story, we will discuss them. Most of these ways follow the philosophy of Total Quality Management (TQM). This philosophy, originally developed for use in the business community, has helped us successfully manage student behavior by creating a new culture at our school—one of co-operation, teamwork, and innovation.

JUDI CALL, Second Grade Teacher
BETH ZIECHECK, Second Grade Teacher
JANICE WRIGHT, Third Grade Teacher
KEN RIGSBY, Fifth Grade Teacher
Rawlings Elementary School
Pinellas Park, Florida

What Is Total Quality Management?

First articulated by American statistician W. Edwards Deming, TQM can, among other things, be defined as a process of improving the quality of organizational activities by changing *systems* rather than changing *people*. TQM can also be considered:

improvement
• a series of small steps toward a better way of working.
• management by leading, not by coercion.

For many educators, TQM has provided a philosophical and practical basis for a new system that can make the continual improvement of schools possible. As teachers begin to see themselves as managers of their own portion of the system and begin to internalize quality principles, they will begin to see new cultures develop in their classrooms—cultures characterized by continuous improvement.

How Do You Implement TQM?

The process described in the following pages is based on our preparation and experiences at Rawlings Elementary. It loosely follows the Plan-Do-Study-Act cycle illustrated on Discipline Reproducible 1.1. This cycle was adapted from its business counterpart—the Shewhart Cycle. The purpose of both TQM cycles is to help implement changes (in this case, mostly behavior changes) smoothly and effectively.

Laying the Groundwork

How does this process begin? On the first day of school, even before making class rules, every classroom drafts a mission statement and class goals.

We've realized that it isn't enough for students to have a mission and goals. They also need to know what is and is not their job at school.

• a cycle of planning, doing, studying, and acting on data for improvement of processes
• breakthrough thinking focusing on the possibilities and opportunities for

We believe that knowing what direction we and our students want to go as a class will influence how we proceed in the learning environment. (See accompanying sidebar for sample mission statement.)

We've also come to realize that it isn't enough for students to have a mission and goals. They also need to know what is and is not their job at school. So we ask them to make a list of what constitutes their job as students and what constitutes the teacher's job.

We spend the next few days of school fine-tuning our lists of roles. With each additional job, we discuss which related actions are the job of the teacher and which are the job of the student. This is important background work because we find that most management problems can then be dealt with later by using one of two simple questions: Are you helping to achieve our mission? Is that your job?

We also include parents in this planning stage. During our school's open house, we share our lists of student and teacher roles. We then take this activity a step farther and develop a list of parent jobs. This helps parents know what their children and their children's teachers expect and need from them.

Once we've completed the job lists for everyone, it's a simple task for teachers and students to derive some rules from these lists. Actually, we think of these as *responsibilities* rather than rules. The way we see it, students need to realize that, although education is a right, it is also a privilege that requires responsible behavior.

In each classroom, we display the class's mission statement, goals, jobs, and responsibilities on charts. Throughout the year, we refer students to these charts whenever they need a quick review or reminder. We have found that time taken at the beginning of the year to establish these expectations is time well spent.

Incorporating Daily Planning

The structure of our school environment allows students to make choices that will help them reach the goals they have set to become better learners. Through classroom dialogue, we collectively set broad goals and then narrow them down to set more specific individual goals. The process begins slowly and simply with repeated modeling and coaching. It then progresses to meet the changing needs of the students as they make those needs known.

This idea follows the basic needs articulated by William Glasser as part of his Control Theory. According to Glasser, every human being has basic needs to belong, gain power, have fun, and be free. In the classroom, we ask our children to make choices that help them become responsible for their behavior. Because all of their behavior takes them either closer to or farther from their goals, they need plans. We establish these plans with the help of daily and/or weekly planning sheets. These sheets vary from teacher to teacher. Discipline Reproducibles 1.2 through

1.4 provide some samples. Basically, students write down what they are expected to do for the following day or week. At the end of each day, they then write down their accomplishments. As needs change and the children become more familiar with the process, planning forms change accordingly.

Our school day includes an "Integrated Workshop" during which the children choose from a variety of curriculum materials and activities. During this time period, the children first reflect on the previous day's plans and evaluate results; they then use these reflections to determine what they will do during the current workshop.

In the classroom, we ask our children to make choices that help them become responsible for their behavior.

Throughout the day, if there are children who don't behave independently, the teacher will say, "How is your behavior helping you to get to your goal? Let's take a look at your plan." This question is posed to all children as a model of what they should ask themselves. The resulting dialogue helps them identify needs and guides them toward productive ways of fulfilling those needs.

We also use evaluation sheets (see Reproducible 1.5 for a sample) to help all students reflect on their plans.

Using Consensus to Deal with Behavior Problems

Many teachers at Rawlings use the class meeting as a way of enabling students to become more responsible for solving their own behavior problems. (It is a particularly effective tool for dealing with petty arguments and tattling among students.)

The procedure is simple. Students place their name on an agenda whenever they have a problem (with their behavior or with someone else's). Weekly class meetings begin with each student complimenting someone. Then, as names are called from the agenda, students present their behavior problem, providing additional information if the situation is unclear. Students discuss the problem and arrive at consequences (action plans), and take a vote.

When we first instituted this process, the majority vote ruled. Today, however, we try to reach consensus on all decisions. Why? Because although "majority rule" allows students to participate, it still makes some students feel like winners and some like losers. "Problem children," who have never been taught to seek or consider alternative solutions, never grow under this system. Once again, they leave punished or reprimanded, but with no clue as to how to modify their behavior.

When consensus replaces majority rule, however, and action plans replace punishments as consequences, students are given a way to grow. The meeting becomes a time for suggesting alternative solutions and exploring justice. All students know that they must agree or, at the very least, signal that "they can live with the consequence." The power of a majority-rule meeting is dissipated; instead, students spend time considering the feelings of the whole class.

Consequences fall into three major categories: a direct (private) apology, a written apology, and a problem solver. Unlike the other two consequences, problem solvers require parental involvement: an important distinction in the minds of students. Problem solvers (see Discipline Reproducible 1.6 for a model form) are taken home and action plans developed from them by the student and a parent. Students reserve this form for repeat offenses or for situations in which someone refuses to apologize to a classmate. Problem solvers keep the parent informed and involved, but do not carry the stigma of a "bad" note. Parents' response has been excellent; they appreciate a system designed to help their children find better cop-

ing behaviors.

Class meetings have handled behavior so successfully that our standard response to minor problems has become "Put it on the agenda." Major altercations will always require a teacher's immediate attention; class meetings will not alter that responsibility. However, many of the annoying interruptions during the course of the day have ceased, the children's ability to solve their own problems has increased, and our class uses the compliment session as a time to reflect and celebrate our growth together.

Facilitating Cooperative Learning and Group Decision Making

We also use the consensus process to implement instruction. In some of our classrooms, children must

articulate a plan of work before they begin any group activity. Materials are placed before them

and the task is explained. The members of each group must then agree on how they will distribute

Advice for TQM Novices

If you are just starting school-based change efforts and would like to "borrow" from the Total Quality Management philosophy, the following guidelines might help you.

1. **Give yourself time.**
   Change doesn't happen quickly.
2. **Start small.**
   Don't try everything at once. Choose one method/activity to try first.
3. **Find support.**
   Find someone else who is willing to try new things. Share your successes and failures.
4. **Communicate with your students' parents.**
   Include them in your planning and training.
5. **Read, read, read.**
   There are many wonderful books to help you along your path to change. (See the Selected Resources at the back of this book.)
6. **Reflect on your definition of discipline.**
   Put your thoughts in writing. From time to time, review and reassess those thoughts.
7. **Ask yourself, "Who's doing the work here?"**
   Your students need to self-assess, plan, and assume responsibility.
8. **Make sure the change you are considering meets your needs.**
   It shouldn't just be something that works for someone else and looks good.
9. **Include your students from the start.**
   It's the best way to promote group ownership in the change.
10. **Keep a journal of the process.**
    It will help you to step back and take a good look at your successes.

the materials, divide the work, and clean up. When the teacher confirms that they truly have reached consensus, they begin.

Although this process may sound simple, conflict can result when confusion develops between two questions: Is it going to be done my way? and Can I live with any other process? Strong-willed (often very bright) students who usually suc-

solutions that take everyone's views into consideration. In the beginning, the teacher suggests a way of proceeding after students have identified the barriers that prevent the group from reaching consensus. However, students cannot rely on a teacher to routinely solve their problems on a routine basis. Ultimately, all groups find consensus a workable process—they tire of be-

group activity we debrief. We tell what went well and where we ran into problems. Often, this is the time when students learn alternative ways of solving their problems; they also realize that there are many acceptable ways to accomplish their tasks.

You might ask yourself if this process is worth the time. Certainly teachers can give specific directions in less time and get on with the task at hand. But remember that we are teaching a skill that will serve our students all their lives. They are learning to consider the views of all members of the group, realizing that each person has a responsibility to do his or her part, analyzing the process with an eye toward improvement, and experiencing the satisfaction of accomplishment through group effort.

Promoting Self-Assessment

In a TQM context, students are not only expected to be responsible for their behavior but also for assessing their learning. They do this by maintaining portfolios and discussing them in student-led conferences every grading period.

In preparing for a conference, students review their portfolios to summarize what they have learned during the grading period. They record this information on a guide sheet (see Discipline Reproducible 1.7 for a sample) that we provide them. Students also use the sheet to help them evaluate their learning goals and gauge the progress they've made toward meeting them.

During the actual conference, the dialogue is

When consensus replaces majority rule, and action plans replace punishments as consequences, students are given a way to grow.

ceed at telling the group what to do suddenly find that this power is gone and that they must find

ing the last to begin and see the practical value in learning to work together.

At the end of each

School Overview

Pinellas County School District is committed to using continuous quality improvement to challenge students to be successful members of America's diverse society. Opened in 1992, Marjorie Kinnan Rawlings Elementary is part of the district's initiative to develop "Total Quality Schools."

Most of Pinellas County's 851,000 residents live in the Tampa-St. Petersburg-Clearwater metropolitan area, one of the fastest-growing metro areas in the United States. With a student population of about 97,000 who are taught in 116 schools, the Pinellas County School District is one of the largest districts in the country.

Located in Pinellas Park, a municipality of about 43,000 people, Rawlings Elementary has about 850 students in pre-kindergarten through fifth grade. Rawlings is a zoned school where about 59 percent of the students receive free or reduced-price lunches. Professional development periods for the staff are built into the school week: teachers participate in a three-hour weekly seminar that allows them the time to learn and study new teaching methods. The focus is on integrating the curriculum through process writing. Recent advances include the provision of instruction to students with special needs in the regular classroom.

During the 1992-93 school year, Rawlings was recognized by the U.S. Department of Education as a "Break the Mold School," and received the Sterling Award for Quality from Florida's governor.

---

between the parent and the child—not between the teacher and the parent. The students share the portfolio and any other work and information of importance as well as what they have written on their guide sheets about personal goals and accomplishments. The student must answer any questions a parent asks. Interestingly enough, most students speak with confidence during the conference because they are able to talk about what they want their parents to know.

Following the conference, the parents are asked to tell their child what they learned from the conference. Most parents like this approach because it enables their child to share school activities with them. For some parents, it gives them some one-to-one time that they don't usually have with their child. Parents also like allowing the child to establish and assess his or her own goals. They realize that children are very aware of their own strengths and weaknesses, and of what they need to do to improve.

Closing Thoughts

The earlier we empower our students to be responsible for their actions and education, the sooner we will see them making the wise choices that will securely qualify them as the leaders of the future. Like growing numbers of teachers and school systems, we feel that realigning systems, rather than trying to reshape students to fit systems, will help our children make that future a satisfying one.◆

The PDSA (Plan-Do-Study-Act) Form
You can use the following action plan to promote appropriate behavior and solve behavior problems.

PLAN

What is our class mission?
What standards do we need to live by in our classroom
to make our mission a reality?
What can we do as a group if any of us falls below the standard?
Have we agreed to standards that we can all live by?
What data can we collect to help guide our decisions?

ACT

Act on the group
decisions.
Be accountable to
someone for your actions.
Continue to gather data
on behavior trends.

Cooperative Group Behavior Management

DO

Meet as a group
to compliment each other
and help each other.
Address agenda items.
Develop a solution
to problems by consensus,
if possible.

STUDY

Have we used this process to help our group?
Have we used this process to help individuals?
Were our decisions reasonable?
What does the data tell us about trends in our classroom behavior?
Are we continually making progress toward our class mission?

Adapted from W. A. Shewhart, *Statistical Method from the Viewpoint of Quality Control* (Washington, D.C.: U.S. Department of Agriculture, 1939, 45.)

Plan Sheet (Sample #1)

Name: _____ Date: _____

What I will do today: _____
_____
_____

Why: _____
_____
_____

What I did today: _____
_____
_____

Why: _____
_____
_____

Self-Evaluation: _____
_____

Plan Sheet (Sample #2)

Name: _____ Date: _____

Plan for the Week

	Plan	Results
Monday		
Tuesday		
Wednesday		
Thursday		
Friday		

Plan Sheet (Sample #3)

Name: _____ Date: _____

	Mon.	Tues.	Wed.	Thurs.	Fri.
Math					
Information					
Reading					
Writing					
Spelling					
Art					
Computer					
Library					

Things I liked:

_____

_____

_____

_____

_____

_____

Things I did not like:

_____

_____

_____

_____

_____

_____

Evaluation Form: How Am I Doing?

Name: _____ Date: _____

Directions: Use this form to evaluate your weekly plans. Get comments from a friend, teacher, and parent.

Student:_____

_____

_____

_____

Friend:_____

_____

_____

Parent:_____

_____

_____

Teacher:_____

_____

_____

Problem Solver Form

Name: _____ Date: _____

1. What happened? _____
_____

2. What did I do? _____
_____

3. How do I feel about it now? _____
_____

- -

Items 4, 5, and 6 to be completed by student and parent.

4. What could I have done differently? _____
_____

5. What will I do the next time? _____
_____

6. Do I owe someone an apology? _____ What should I say? _____
_____

_____   _____
Student's Signature   *Parent's Signature*

Student-Led Conference: A Guide Sheet

Name: _____ **Date:** _____

My goal for this last grading period was: _____

_____

My plan for achieving this goal was: _____

_____

I did/did not meet my goal because: _____

_____

Some things I learned during this grading period are: _____

_____

Some things I still need to work on are: _____

_____

My new goal for the next grading period is: _____

_____

My plan for achieving this goal is: _____

_____

Reader Reflections

Insights: _____

_____

_____

_____

_____

Actions for Our School (District) to Consider: _____

_____

_____

_____

_____

_____

_____

PLAYGROUND PEACEMAKERS

This Idaho elementary school uses student mediators to settle most playground disputes.

2 "Sara pushed me!" Steve whines.

"Do you want to solve this with the duty teacher or with the conflict managers?" a teacher asks.

"The conflict managers. Because otherwise, I get a playground violation!" Sara says.

The duty teacher signals to the conflict managers (CMs), who soon arrive at the scene of the dispute.

One of the CMs asks, "Do you both agree with the four rules of resolving conflict? They are: 1) agree to solve the problem, 2) be as honest as you can, 3) no put-downs, and 4) no interrupting. Do you agree?"

"Yes, I guess so." Sara says.

"Do you also agree?" the CM asks Steve.

Steve nods.

Steve seems angrier than Sara, so the CMs ask him to speak first. "Please tell us what happened, Steve," one CM asks.

"Well, I was just standing in line, waiting for the bell to ring, and Sara pushed me for no reason at all. I bumped into Brian and scraped my arm on the brick wall! And now even Brian's mad at me!"

"So, what you're saying is that Sara pushed you while you were in line, and you bumped someone else and hurt your arm. Is that correct?"

DONNA JOHNSON and MARCY EISELE

Fifth Grade Teachers
Orchards Elementary School
Lewiston, Idaho

Steve says yes.

The CM then turns to Sara. "Now, Sara, it's your turn. Tell us what happened in your words."

"I didn't push him, and I don't know how he hurt his arm. He's a creep!" she shouts.

The CM steps in, saying, "You agreed not to use put-downs."

"Well," continues Sara, "I didn't do anything, anyway!"

Steve begins to break in; the CM quickly reminds him that he had agreed not to interrupt.

The CM restates what Sara had said, and Sara

nods in agreement.

"Steve, how does this make you feel?" the CM asks.

"I feel mad, and my arm hurts!" he says.

"Sara, how do you feel about what has happened?"

"I feel OK, because I didn't do anything!" she replies.

The CM asks Sara how she may have become involved in the pushing in-

Conflict resolution shows students that they can communicate feelings by using active listening and clear speaking techniques.

cident. She finally says, "Well, maybe Steve was in the way when my friend and I were playing a shov-

ing game. I guess maybe he got pushed by accident."

The CM asks both parties, "What do you think you can do to make it better and to keep it from happening again?"

"Well," Steve begins, "Sara could leave this school and never come back!"

The CM asks Sara if she could agree to that. Of course, the answer is "NO!"

The CM asks Steve if he has any other ideas, and Steve suggests that maybe Sara could stay away from him whenever they are in line.

Sara responds, "Sure, but I still didn't mean to hurt him!"

The CMs say, "Congratulations, you have just solved your problem," and they shake hands with both parties.

You have just relived

an actual playground conflict that students at Orchards Elementary in Lewiston, Idaho, successfully resolved themselves. As a matter of fact, students at Orchards Elementary use conflict resolution skills to handle most playground disputes themselves.

Our school staff believes that conflict is an ordinary occurrence and that students are capable of finding peaceful solutions to their problems. As a result, we teach conflict resolution skills to all students, at all grade levels (K-6). We also select and train certain students to be conflict managers (CMs) on the playground. Their task is to help other students find positive ways to resolve minor disagreements during recess. (Please note: CMs *do not* mediate physical fights

between students!)

How It All Started

Orchards Elementary is one of seven elementary schools in Lewiston, Idaho. The school has an enrollment of 322 and is part of Lewiston Independent School District #1.

Conflict resolution came to Orchards Elementary in the late 1980s. During this time, our school joined 25 schools across the United States to become part of the National Education Association's Mastery in Learning Project. Through this project, we were to design a teacher-driven school improvement process. As we worked through the project, we discovered that we on the Orchards Elementary staff lacked some of the skills needed to resolve conflicts within our own professional peer groups.

When a professor from the University of Idaho approached us to serve as a research study for his thesis on conflict resolution in schools, we quickly recognized the opportunity this offer presented to us—as well as to our students. The professor shared information from another conflict resolution project and invited us to pilot a similar program that would train both teachers and students.

Our teacher-training sessions with the professor included lessons in listening skills, how to read body language, paraphrasing, and other communication techniques.

Early Buy-In

To help convince our colleagues to "buy into" conflict resolution, we made sure to introduce the concept to everyone on the school staff and to discuss the program with them. In introducing the program, we used manuals from the School Initiatives Program of the Community Board Center for Policy and Training. (See Reproducible 2.4 for address and phone number.)

Our principal supported the idea and was directly involved every step of the way. He helped us get the funds we needed to purchase training materials for teachers and T-shirts for student CMs. He also found money to pay release time for and stipends to the teachers who would complete intensive training in conflict resolution and then train other teachers and all of the CMs.

Initial Student Training

When we first introduced the student component,
teachers selected students in the fourth through sixth grades to serve as CMs on the playground during morning, lunch, and afternoon recesses. These were students who had shown that they were responsible, dependable, and trustworthy. We've since found that competent CMs can come in all behavioral styles, from the goody-two-shoes type to the playground bully who knows every trick in the book! Today, the requirements are more open: A prospective CM must have the desire to be a CM and must successfully complete a rigorous training program.

Peer mediators learn many skills before they are put on the job. First, they learn how to listen carefully, restate and clarify what they hear, and ask neutral yet pertinent

questions. They then learn how to shift through differing perceptions to the underlying cause of a conflict, how to defuse anger, and how to develop empathy between the disputants. Finally, they learn to maintain confidentiality (unless they hear allegations of abuse or threats of violence—then they must report this information to a teacher). This initial training can take approximately 15 to 20 hours.

Our first half-day training session included 50 to 60 students and three teachers. We soon discovered, though, that it's far more effective to train only 20 to 25 students (along with two or three teachers) at a time.

Today's Training Methods

At first, we did CM training once a year. We now train about 20 fourth graders in the fall as well as a handful of fifth graders. Then we retrain all the conflict managers sometime early in the second semester to hone their skills and renew their motivation.

Each year, we also try to teach a few basic lessons in conflict resolution to

Some students have even told us that they use conflict resolution techniques at home!

every student in each grade level. These lessons cover communication topics such as listening, under-standing other persons' points of view, and para-phrasing.

When the fourth graders receive their fall semester training (with veteran fifth graders as partners), this marks the beginning of a one-year "apprentice-ship."

We have discovered that our fifth graders are the linchpins of our conflict manager program because they have had one year of experience, are not as in-timidated by the "big sixth graders," and usually are highly motivated. We elevate the top quality CMs to "captain" status when they reach sixth grade (each month we designate two different sixth graders to be the captains).

This process of ad-vancement gives every CM something to look for-ward to next year.

Standard Procedures

We begin each week with a meeting in the fifth grade classroom of the teacher advisor (Donna Johnson). At these meet-ings, students sign up with the partner they wish to work with and in-dicate whether some days are better for them to work than others. Each CM works approximately two days a month. Using this information, the advi-sor makes up a monthly schedule and gives each CM a copy.

In addition, at our week-ly meetings we discuss problems we encounter on the playground. For in-stance, some teachers solve problems them-selves without offering students the CM option, and some teachers forget to give the CMs their daily reward—Panther Paws, our

school's good-behavior tokens.

We also role-play the correct way to be a conflict manager under various difficult situations, such as when a kindergarten student cries, "Me want the DUTY!" (the teacher on duty), or when stu-dents simply fail to reach successful resolution of a problem. Finally, we dis-cuss the importance of the job of being a CM, which gives everyone the oppor-tunity to tell his or her most recent playground "story" to peers who can empathize, advise, ap-plaud, and/or encourage.

Each day commences with the two sixth grade captains coming into the advisor's classroom and checking to see who is on duty. Before school be-gins, the captains make sure to leave reminders on the desks of the students

who will be the CMs that day. Promptly at 9 a.m., the captains announce the names of the day's conflict managers over the intercom. At each recess, the CMs don fluorescent lime-green vests trimmed in black with CONFLICT MANAGER printed on the back, and pick up their clipboards with a form to be filled out for each conflict. At the end of the day, they receive, in addition to their Panther Paws, a conflict manager paw.

The reward system for the CMs has developed on the basis of trial and error. It was evident from the beginning that being a conflict manager was different from working in the kitchen during lunch hours or being on the safety patrol. The big difference was that being a CM would take up all of a student's recess time for an entire day.

Faced with that requirement, we decided that we would begin by making the job a prestigious one. That is why we announce the CMs of the day over the intercom, post pictures of "CMs of the Month" on the school bulletin board, provide treats at the weekly CM meetings, allow CMs to design their own uniforms, and conduct a pizza and pop party for them at the end of the school year.

Conclusion

Our school staff believes that conflict is an ordinary occurrence and that students are capable of finding peaceful solutions to their problems. As students learn to solve their own problems, they learn to become responsible people.

We don't even begin to pretend that all our problems have disappeared at Orchards Elementary. However, the number of conflicts on the playground has fallen. The number of "green slips" given for playground misconduct has also dramatically decreased. The playground duty staff report that every day they see children resolving their own disagreements, leaving the staff free to handle problems of a more serious nature such as physical fights and accidents.

Observations by teachers and comments by the principal also support the impression that our students' ability to solve their own problems has improved. Some students have even told us that they use conflict resolution techniques at home!

Although our conflict resolution program has its

Spreading the Word

People living in Independent School District #1, the Lewiston area, and even beyond, have learned about the conflict resolution program at Orchards Elementary through a number of ways. We have

• sent brochures home to parents;

• made presentations at PTA events, teachers' conferences, and statewide university and business conferences;

• made presentations on our program to other school faculties in our district and have invited them to observe us when we do training;

• received exposure from the print and electronic media at the local, state, and national levels.

imperfections, we firmly believe that without the program we would still be solving conflicts between students the old-fashioned way: The teacher or the principal would mete out the consequences, logical or not, and the kids would not know how to "talk out" their problems.

Instead, we *all* have been enriched by our peer mediation program—the staff, the parents, the community, and most of all, our kids. ◆

The Four Rules of Conflict Resolution

1 Agree to solve the problem.

2 Be as honest as you can.

3 Do not use put-downs.

4 Do not interrupt.

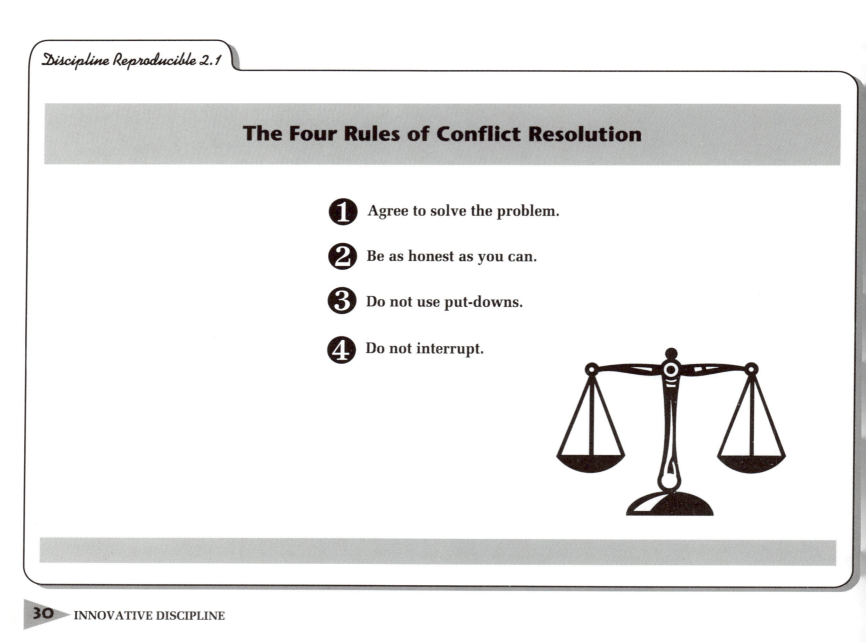

Conflict Manager Report Form

Conflict Managers _____ **Date** _____

_____

Who had the conflict? _____   _____

_____   _____

What type of conflict was it? ☐ Argument ☐ Fight ☐ Rumor ☐ Other _____

How did you find out about it? ☐ Student ☐ Administrator ☐ Teacher ☐ Aide ☐ Counselor ☐ Yourself

What was the conflict about? _____

_____

_____

Was the conflict resolved? ☐ Yes ☐ No

Resolution:

_____ agrees to :   _____ agrees to:
(Student's name)   (Student's name)

_____   _____

_____   _____

Ways to Encourage Student Involvement In a Conflict Manager Program

Every time a student serves as a conflict manager, that student gives up all recess time for that particular day. To help motivate students with CM potential to get involved, and stay involved, despite this great sacrifice, you may want to institute some of these actions in your school. These motivators add prestige to the CM job.

- Announce the CMs for the day on the school intercom.

- Announce the names of new CMs at a schoolwide assembly.

- Post photos of "CMs of the Month" on the school bulletin board.

- Provide treats at CM meetings.

- Give the CMs a say in how their uniforms are designed.

- Give a party for the CMs at the end of the school year.

Organizations That Can Assist Your School With Conflict Resolution

Children's Creative Response to Conflict Program, Fellowship of Reconciliation, Box 271, Nyack, NY 10960, (914) 358-4601.

Community Board Program, 1540 Market St., Ste. 490, San Francisco, CA 94102, voice (415) 552-1250, fax (415) 626-0595.

Educators for Social Responsibility, School Conflict Resolution Programs, 23 Garden St., Cambridge, MA 02138, (617) 492-1764.

National Association for Mediation in Education, 205 Hampshire House, Box 33635, Amherst, MA 01003-3635, (415) 545-2462.

Network on Conflict Resolution, Association for Supervision and Curriculum Development, Attn. Mary Ellen Schaffer, Assistant Principal, Elsie Johnson School, 1380 Nautilus Lane, Hanover Park, IL 60103, voice (708) 830-8770, fax (708) 893-5452.

Northwest Mediation Service, 405 11-4th Ave., Bellevue, WA 98004, (208) 455-3989.

School Initiatives Program of the Community Board Center for Policy and Training, 149 Ninth St., San Francisco, CA 94103, (415) 552-1250.

Reader Reflections

Insights: _____

_____

_____

_____

_____

Actions for Our School (District) to Consider: _____

_____

_____

_____

_____

_____

_____

Our school staff believes that conflict is an ordinary occurrence and that students are capable of finding peaceful solutions to their problems.

A JUSTICE SYSTEM OF THEIR OWN

Members of a student-run court handle minor discipline disturbances at this Kentucky middle school.

3 I teach seventh grade social studies at Lassiter Middle School in Louisville, Kentucky. Lassiter serves approximately 874 students in grades six through eight. It is part of the Jefferson County Public School System, which is the seventeenth largest school district in the United States. Our learning team, Pacesetters: The Next Generation, is composed of five teachers, Patricia Noe (math teacher and team leader), Sarah Rudolph and June Lee (reading and writing teachers), Juli Koch (science teacher), and me. We have approximately 150 seventh grade students on our team. They are grouped heterogeneously into five classes.

Out of Frustration Comes Inspiration

I had always considered Lassiter a great place to work, but a few years ago, I became more and more frustrated over the amount of instructional time I lost dealing with petty classroom disturbances. Because I was very interested in law, I decided to establish a student court that would handle these minor problems. I used both trial and error and student suggestions to set up this peer-group judicial system, which basically emulates the American system of justice. I called it the Review Board, and it has been effective to this day.

Review Board Training

To pique interest in this peer-driven justice system, I teach a beginning law class that covers legal terms, arrest and courtroom procedures, and students' basic constitutional rights. Although the class is helpful to students who become members of the Review Board, attendance is not a prerequisite. Any student who meets the following criteria can apply to serve on the Re-

FRONDA YANCY

Seventh Grade Social Studies Teacher

Lassiter Middle School

Louisville, Kentucky

view Board:
- submission of a letter explaining the student's reasons for wanting to be a member
- a good attendance record
- passing grades.

The size of the Review Board's meeting room dictates that no more than 40 students can serve on the board, so from a large pool of applicants, I select eight students from each homeroom to be board members. During this se-

Not all students selected for the Review Board have A averages and perfect conduct.

lection process, I make an effort to strike an appropriate racial and gender balance.

I should point out that not all students selected for the Review Board have A averages and perfect conduct. Quite the contrary, some members are known to have occasional problems with grades and behavior. Being a Review Board member has improved the conduct of such board members because they know if they are referred to the Review Board for misconduct, they face a double penalty.

As sponsor of the student court, I give students the initial training for their service on the Review Board. After this orientation, students train other students throughout the school year to do different jobs in our student justice system.

If a student wants to leave the Review Board or is voted off by the rest of the board, I select some-

one to take his or her place. Reasons for being voted off the board include poor grades, chronic discipline problems, and violations of the Review Board Creed—in particular its confidentiality requirements. (See the accompanying sidebar for the text of the Review Board Creed.) Dismissed board members who show improvement in problem areas may be voted back onto the board.

How the Review Board Works

The Review Board meets every school day during a 40-minute counseling period that has been built into the daily schedule at Lassiter. Students are referred to the board by teachers for minor infractions of the school rules (e.g., being at one's locker

at the wrong time, being unprepared for class, showing disrespect, being tardy). The student appears before the Review Board, having signed a referral to the board from his or her teacher and having agreed to abide by the board's verdict. I attend all proceedings in my capacity as sponsor to ensure that all students' rights are respected—those of board members as well as those of the accused. Any student found guilty of an infraction is assigned a probation officer who oversees the student's "rehabilitation."

The Review Board is staffed by students who serve in the following capacities:
- The *chairperson* calls the meeting to order and presides over the proceedings.
- The *bailiff* reads referrals to the board, sees that

he proceedings don't run overtime, and leads the board members in reciting the Review Board Creed at the beginning of each meeting.

A staff of four *secretaries* is responsible for keeping accurate records of all students who appear before the board; for taking minutes of each meeting; for reading the previous day's minutes to the board; for drawing up passes that, along with the sponsor's signature, enable a student who has appeared before the board to return to class; for calling roll; and for keeping track of the attendance of board members.

• An *usher* escorts defendants in and out of the hearing room and makes sure that unauthorized persons do not enter the room while a hearing is in progress.

• A *keeper* is responsible for staying with and supervising defendants who are waiting outside to appear before the board.

• Two or three *runners* make sure all students who have been referred to the board are at their hearing at the appropriate time. The runners bring the students from class, one at a time, to appear before the board. The defendant stays outside with the keeper until his or her case is called.

• *Probation officers* are responsible for ensuring that students found guilty of an offense are completing their punishments; the probation officer reports to the board daily on students' progress.

• *Board members* represent all homerooms on the team. With the exception of the keeper, whose duties keep him or her out-side the hearing room, all 40 board members, even if serving that day in another capacity such as secretary or usher, hear the case and vote on the verdict.

Members of the Review Board rotate to a different job every week.

The Review Board's motto is "Commit the crime; pay the time." More often than not, students assign a punishment that relates to the crime. For example, a student found guilty of failing to bring a required book to class might be sentenced to carry all of his or her books around each day for a week, with no locker breaks. A probation officer is assigned to make sure the student is indeed doing this. All sentences are voted on by the board; similar offenses tend to draw similar sentences. Disciplinary action for se-

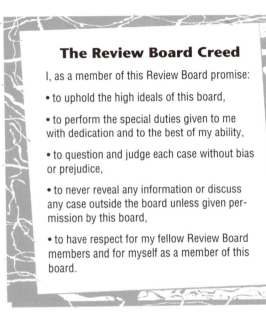

The Review Board Creed

I, as a member of this Review Board promise:

• to uphold the high ideals of this board,

• to perform the special duties given to me with dedication and to the best of my ability,

• to question and judge each case without bias or prejudice,

• to never reveal any information or discuss any case outside the board unless given permission by this board,

• to have respect for my fellow Review Board members and for myself as a member of this board.

rious offenses remain the responsibility of the school administration.

Students are not always found guilty. In one instance, a student was charged with being late to class. His teacher gave him a punishment, but later referred him to the Review Board as well. The board dismissed the charges on the grounds that he had already been punished. In another instance, the Review Board found a student innocent whom the referring teacher considered guilty. Having been present when the case was tried, I spoke to the teacher on behalf of the Review Board, explaining that information had come to light to clear the student of the charge. The teacher subsequently accepted the board's decision.

The administration at Lassiter Middle School constantly encourages teachers to try new things

The Review Board's motto is "Commit the crime; pay the time."

even if success is not always assured. In keeping with this policy, I have always received support from the school's principal, counselor, and teachers. In fact, our principal, Fred Harbison, believes that by letting the Review Board take care of minor disciplinary problems within the Pacesetters: The Next Generation team, he can devote more time to teacher needs, classroom visits, and curriculum. He sees the Review Board as a means of empowering students while addressing discipline problems in an innovative way.

Teachers on my team have commented on the changes in students' behavior since the conception of the Review Board, and teachers on other teams at Lassiter have incorporated Review Boards into their own discipline strategies.

Parents also seem favorably disposed toward the Review Board.

How the Review Board Has Evolved

Each year, the Review Board goes through changes. One year, we added the creed; another year, we changed the length of time each student stays in a specific job. We've added "down times" on Fridays when we do other law-related activities. These include field trips to state courts, presentations by guest speakers such as judges and police officers, mock trials, and discussions of certain crimes being committed by young people in the Louisville area.

One of the most important things I've learned in dealing with the students on the Review Board is that, to be effective, students must have a feeling of ownership and pride in being an active member.

I've tried to encourage thi in the following ways:
• by having students elec to serve, rather than b appointed to the Review Board
• by supplying Review Board T-shirts
• by arranging for a group picture in the school yearbook
• by encouraging members of the board to eat lunch together and opt to leave lunch five minutes early in order to prepare for the day's cases
• by sharing with board members all forms of positive recognition of their activities
• by telling board members on every possible occasion how proud I am of their dedication and accomplishments.

Per the Review Board Creed, students must keep board business confidential unless given permis-

sion by fellow board members to do otherwise. This policy gives members the freedom to speak frankly and uncover the information they need to reach a fair verdict.

Like any justice system, our student court occasionally makes mistakes. (As noted earlier, the sponsor is always present at proceedings to ensure that no injustice is done and that proper procedures are followed.) If the board members or the sponsor feel dissatisfied with the board's performance in a certain instance, we talk. Usually, we can iron out our differences of opinion via discussion and compromise.

In instances when the members of the Review Board feel that the student justice process has been unable to make a positive impact on a defendant,

that student is referred back to the team teachers.

How We Know It's Working

Although I have never conducted a written survey to see if our Review Board is making a difference in student conduct, I can tell by comparing the abundance of cases we get at the beginning of the school year to the scarcity of cases that occur by the latter part of the year that the board does have a positive effect. By spring, I find myself *almost* wishing we had more cases.

I think another indicator of our success is the fact that there's always a long list of students waiting to become members of the Review Board. When asked why he wanted to be on the board, one student said he thought that the student court would be fun

Lassiter Middle School Review Board Procedures

1. Roll call

2. Review Board called to order

3. Reading of the Review Board Creed

4. Reading of the minutes of the previous meeting

5. Presentation of the case

6. Questioning by the Review Board (After the questioning, the defendant leaves the room.)

7. Discussion by the Review Board

8. Vote on the verdict

9. Discussion of punishment, if the defendant is found guilty. A probation officer is assigned at this time.

10. Motion to report to the defendant

11. The defendant returns and receives the board's decision. The defendant is asked if he or she understands the verdict and the punishment. Once the defendant says yes, he or she signs a summary of the proceedings. Copies go to the referring teacher and the probation officer. The probation officer signs this paper when the punishment is completed.

12. Probation officer report

13. Old and new business

14. Adjournment

and would be a different way to learn. Another commented that the student court seemed exciting and would be like nothing she had ever done before. Another student, although eager to serve, said that one thing she didn't like about the Review Board is that sometimes you have to try your friends, and you can't go easy on them because the creed requires

you to judge each case without bias or prejudice.

One board member perhaps best summarized the appeal—and the value—of service on the Review Board when she said that she really enjoyed doing her board job because having to be there and do a job right gave her a feeling of responsibility.◆

Guidelines for an Effective Review Board

1. See that members of the Review Board meet every day. This is not only good for the board as an organization, but also honors students' right to a "speedy trial."

2. Establish guidelines for admission to the Review Board that average students can attain.

3. Always let students volunteer to be on the Review Board, rather than appoint them. Once they are members, allow them to volunteer for jobs.

4. From time to time, plan a "down day" for the Review Board in which students do not try cases but use the time for activities that establish board rapport and a sense of ownership in the student court.

5. As a sponsor, be prepared at the onset to have to sell the idea to your fellow teachers and the administration.

6. Be prepared to work hard. Sponsoring a successful Review Board takes extra hours and extra patience.

Staffing a Review Board

Ask students on the Review Board to volunteer for the following staff positions:

Chairperson
- calls meetings to order
- presides over proceedings.

Bailiff
- reads referrals to the board
- sees that the proceedings don't run overtime
- leads board members in reciting the Review Board creed (if applicable).

Secretaries
- keep records of all students appearing before the board
- take minutes of each meeting
- read the previous day's minutes to the board
- draw up passes that, along with the sponsor's signature, enable a defendant to return to class
- call roll
- keep track of the attendance of board members.

Keeper
- stays with and supervises defendants when they wait to appear before the board.

Staffing a Review Board
(Continued)

Usher
- escorts defendants in and out of the hearing room
- makes sure no unauthorized person enters while a hearing is in progress.

Runners
- make sure all students who have been referred to the board are at their hearing at the appropriate time
- bring the defendants from class one at a time to appear before the board.

Board Members
- represent all homerooms on the team
- hear cases
- vote on verdicts and punishments.

Probation Officers
- ensure that students found guilty of an offense are completing their punishments
- report to the board daily on students' progress toward completion of punishments.

Reader Reflections

Insights: _____

_____

_____

_____

_____

_____

Actions for Our School (District) to Consider: _____

_____

_____

_____

_____

_____

_____

_____

_____

HEART TO HEART

Through a biweekly support group called Heart to Heart, sixth graders in this Nashville school learn to handle the type of personal problems that can otherwise lead to discipline problems.

4 Teaching by choice in the inner city for the past 15 years has been a daily test of my flexibility to adapt to each discipline situation and to each student's problems individually. I have spent many "mind-boggling" hours, thinking; rethinking; working; and reworking new plans, approaches, motivations, and rewards that would encourage good behavior.

Today, as a teacher in Metropolitan Nashville Public Schools,

I use several forms of positive motivation at the same time to deter discipline problems within my classroom. I believe there is no such thing as *one way* to work successfully with students, regardless of grade level. Every teacher needs an open mind and a surplus of ideas and ingenuity because every class is different, every student is different, and every discipline problem is different. In this chapter, however, I will discuss one strategy that I have found particularly helpful—that of establishing a support group for students.

Establishing a Support Group

Why a support group? I believe that both adults and children misbehave and draw negative attention to themselves to meet

SUSAN C. ADLER
Sixth Grade Teacher
Tom Joy Elementary School
Nashville, Tennessee

needs that are often ill-attended. Many children are confronted daily with fears, anger, depression, repression, and countless other negative feelings, without validation from the adults in their lives. These children, also, do not know how to deal with these feelings. I have always felt that there are very few truly "bad" children. The "problem children" are usually good children unable to handle their troubles, unwilling or unable to seek adult help, and very protective of the "slugs" in their lives. They disrupt classes, talk rudely to adults, and refuse to complete assignments, but all of these forms of "acting out" are in reality armor to protect the vulnerable child within (such disruptions are termed *defense mechanisms* by many of us).

I decided years ago that my students should have an outlet, both positive and healing, for these feelings. I began to set aside two periods per week to actually have a support group for my students.

young adolescents face.

Last year, teaching fifth grade at Lockeland Middle School, the students decided to name our group Heart to Heart. I plan to continue to use this very special name for years to come. It covers the entire purpose of the group itself. We sit together as equals and talk openly and honestly, trusting each other to respect our various feelings and to keep our talks solely within the group. Confiden-

School, where I teach sixth grade, my students are already so involved in Heart to Heart each Tuesday and Thursday that they enter the room these mornings looking forward to "group" and asking if it is still scheduled.

One afternoon we were deeply into a serious discussion. The classroom door opened and Stella Simpson, our principal, looked into the room intending to say something to me. In unison, several students turned toward the door and exclaimed, "You can't come in here! This is very private!" Mrs. Simpson, being a strong child advocate and knowing my history of having group sessions with my classes, respectfully said, "Oh, please excuse me. I didn't realize you were having your group." She closed the

door quietly and left us to continue our discussion. The students were not being disrespectful toward her, but they were following our procedures and expectations established the first day we met.

Goals for The Group

I have two formal goals for Heart to Heart:

1. to provide a warm, caring environment in order to facilitate personal and academic growth and

2. to provide a support program, based on the group concept, that will help students deal with pre-adolescent problems and concerns in positive, appropriate ways.

Through this group structure, I also hope students will come to realize two things. First, and most important, that there is a way to release pent-up

I want the students to recognize that there is a way to release pent-up anger and pain through talking it out.

During this time we would discuss school-based problems, home conflicts, and many other difficulties

tiality is essential, and the students strictly attend to this rule.

This year at Tom Joy

nger and pain through talking it out. Sometimes, just sharing with others how we feel is like lifting the top off a boiling pot of water. Steam escapes, and the temperature drops; but the water still remains until it evaporates slowly. This is the same with life. We can learn to open our mouths, let out our feelings, feel better inside, and still survive with the problem until it either dissipates or until we learn to accept and to live with it. The problem may not go away, but it can be easier for children to endure it when they have a safe place to talk.

Second, I hope that through the group process, children will come to understand that often they are not responsible for the bad things that affect their lives. Very often they are innocently subjected to adult dysfunctional behavior, and at times, witness horrendous activities. Children sometimes live with alcoholism, drug addiction, family members who deal drugs, prostitution, domestic disputes, child abuse (physical, emotional, and sexual), problematic siblings, poverty, fear of playing outside, gunshots day and night, and so on. Most of the children I have taught in the past years witnessed at least one violent, deadly attack involving adults. Many have blamed themselves for parental problems and have learned through the group how to place the responsibility back on the adults where it really belongs. (This lesson is much more important than remembering the names of explorers in North America!)

Modus Operandi

How does the group operate? First and foremost, a group is only as successful as its facilitator (guide). That guide is you, the teacher! You must be willing to sit down with your class and to let your human side materialize. Just remember, the hardest part for many teachers is giving up the role of "teacher"—sitting down with the class as an equal and sharing personal experiences. We are so accustomed to being serious teachers that sometimes it is easy to forget that the audience before us is composed of children. Children may be six years old or 13 years old. They may be smart-talking, street-wise, and a problem in class; but they are still simply children. For us to sit down with them and talk person to person and,

more important, to listen to them is not a loss of control as a teacher. If anything, it is gaining control through trust, love, and acceptance of our students and vice-versa.

Your role in Heart to Heart is to be your honest self and to follow the same rules of the group as the students. After all, you are not shockable, right? You have either heard it all, read about it, or seen it on TV. You are not there to teach during group. It's okay to speak, and it is okay to give advice. It is not okay to preach values. Listen, listen, and listen!

Let's assume that you are ready to sit down and chat person to person with your class. You are now on your way to experiencing many personal insights into yourself and into your students. You are taking a major step toward really bonding with your students, and therefore, establishing an intimacy built on trust and sharing of inner selves.

Ideally, your class will begin Heart to Heart the first week of school. You will explain the purpose of the group, what the children can expect, the rules, and the fact that

Confidentiality is essential, and the students strictly attend to this rule.

you will also be a member of the group. (Let me interject that if the school year is already in progress,

it is not too late to begin your group. It is beneficial to all even if it is well into the year, so don't wait.)

During the first two sessions, pull up a chair and sit down in a circle with your class. (Note: You may want to do away with the circle after a few sessions.) Explain that in the future when you do this, it will be the signal that Heart to Heart is beginning. It is also the way you will be saying, "I am no longer the teacher but part of our group." These first two sessions may leave your students wondering about what is really happening because to most children this is often a new experience. Tell your class this is going to be an all-year activity meant to bring every member closer together, to give us a time to share concerns and to work out problems as we

talk openly.

During the first session, discuss the following rules. They are meant to provide boundaries and safe feelings within the group.

Rule #1: Everyone is accepted in this group.

Rule #2: Never put-down anyone or laugh at anyone.

Rule #3: Speak what you really feel.

Rule #4: Everyone gets a chance to talk (one by one, around the circle). When it is your turn to talk, you have the option to pass (be quiet).

Rule #5: No one talks about what is said outside the group.

Reiterate that you are simply one member of the group, just as each of them, and there will be times you may want to bring a problem to the group, too. Students love this because suddenly

their "teacher" is really human.

During the second session, I introduce a short discussion where we all participate. I may say, "Let's pretend your life is written in pencil. What is one thing you would erase?" I start out with my own reply, such as, "I would erase the time I lost my temper and hit my sister." Then the next group member usually feels freer to speak up, because I, the teacher, started the discussion. Don't be discouraged if, during the first few meetings, several children say, "I pass." This only verifies that this is either new to them, that they may be shy, or that they may be afraid to trust the group. As the group meets over and over, you will not need to introduce a discussion topic, and children will join in more

and more. Often, the discussions are in full swing when they are forced to end due to time allowance. Students of mine invariably complain when time runs out.

Heart to Heart meets twice each week, but you will discover that children will talk to you or write to you on "off-days" if there is another problem. This is when you realize that you have won their trust. Discipline problems begin to fade, because students are bonding, are talking out problems, are realizing they no longer stand alone, and are actually developing some very sophisticated life skills. They begin to look at alternatives to fighting, to recognize that perhaps we act as we do because of our problems, and to learn to show comfort to peers by hugging or by bringing a tissue to a crying student. As the group proceeds through the school year, I proudly watch leaders emerge from the group who are capable of actually facilitating Heart to Heart. I see quiet students become talkers, and insecure young men and women gain confidence in what they say as being important. I believe one of the greatest joys is observing a solemn, serious student learning to relax and to laugh.

Finding the Time

Recently, a teacher asked me, "How do you find time for your little group?" I told her that I *make time* twice a week, preferably at the end of the day. She then asked, "How do you fit in all the required subjects on those days?" My reply was simply, "I don't. I leave something out, because Heart to Heart is more important." I mean this! As I said previously, it is perhaps the most significant thing I do as a teacher. It sets the tone for positive learning. Through the group, we learn to think, to problem-solve, to organize our thoughts, and to practice positive self-talk. This carries over into the academics and into social interactions outside class and thus de-escalates discipline problems.

Most students do not want to be a problem! They don't want to be in trouble day after day. They don't want to fail. I have learned that most discipline problems are begging to be solved. The disruptive student is indirectly asking to have controls placed on him or her. And, when we take time to do positive controlling, we are essentially saying, "I care about you; that is why I am spending my time on you." In answer to the question about how to fit in Heart to Heart, just do it! Save an academic subject for the next day. It pays off!

...the hardest part for many teachers is giving up the role of "teacher"—sitting down with the class as an equal and sharing personal experiences.

Topics for Discussion

What topics do you discuss in Heart to Heart? In our group, any subject matter is acceptable if it is important to the students. Whether it be problems in the classroom; trouble at home; conflict with peers; or more serious issues such as abuse, chemical dependency, sexual encounters, theft, or any of numerous adolescent problems, we talk about it all.

I always have a topic prepared to present (i.e., usually something in the area of values clarification or self-esteem), but rarely do I need to use it. The group usually is ready to go on its own track of ideas. If I have noticed a particular problem in the class such as students exhibiting racial prejudice, I will often sit down with our group and present *my* problem. I might say, "Group I need your help. I have a problem when I notice some of you calling each other racial names. This upsets me because I do not understand. What do we need to do? What do I need to do to feel better inside?" The students then take over and usually work through the "whys" and usually come up with suggestions on how to improve things. This keeps me from standing up as teacher and ordaining that there will be no more name-calling or whatever, knowing full well that I will be talking to the walls. Students tune out lectures, but will listen and resolve conflicts in discussions when their ideas are respected.

If you are familiar with conflict resolution (see the two previous stories in this book), you will notice some similarities between that form of problem solving and Heart to Heart. I believe that anytime children can solve their own problems with peers and reach mutual agreement, it is growth for all parties involved. We all learn by experiences, good and bad, so I support and use this process every day, too.

Conclusion

When I started this chapter, I said that there is no such thing as one form of positive discipline. Just as an electrician needs several tools, so do we as teachers. I suggest that new teachers as well as those of us who have been in the field awhile learn all types of innovative discipline techniques.

Heart to Heart is not the only solution to today's school problems, but I can tell you it is one of the best ways to prevent many discipline problems. I won't assure you a "perfect classroom" where students are all clones of your expectations and values. You will still have some problems. Heart to Heart will, however, set a firm foundation on which to build a class where all persons are respected as individuals. With this solid foundation, you can begin to facilitate personal and academic growth. Then you can say, "I am really a teacher. With my help, many of my students have learned not only academics but, also, important living skills that will help them to survive in an often not so kind world."◆

Heart-to-Heart Rules

 Everyone is accepted in this group.

 Never put-down anyone or laugh at anyone.

 Speak what you really feel.

 Everyone gets a turn to talk. When it becomes your turn to talk, you have the option to pass (be quiet).

5 Outside the group, no one talks about what is said within the group.

Heart-to-Heart Creed for Teachers

1. I will be a positive person even if I must fake it.

2. I will always keep an open, nonjudgmental state of mind.

3. I will strive to be a good role model for the students.

4. I will respect the confidentiality of members of my group unless it would prove harmful to their or others' well-being.

5. I will practice open and honest communication and encourage other group members to do the same.

6. I will motivate students during all activities.

7. I will review the "ground rules" every time our group meets and be sure they are respected by all members.

8. I will listen a lot and talk only a little.

9. I will plan our sessions fully and make them anything but boring.

10. I will be very flexible and ready to drop all plans if the group or an individual is in need of specific help.

11. I will not expect every session to run smoothly because some will flop.

Heart-to-Heart Creed for Teachers
(Continued)

12. I will constantly try to create an atmosphere within the group where all members may feel comfortable, relaxed, and accepted.

13. I will give good eye contact and not be interruptive.

14. I will allow members to form their own solutions to any problems and resist the "adult" temptation to jump in and impose my own ideas.

15. I will remember my childhood and try to understand theirs.

16. I will not take it upon myself to change all members of the group to conform to my values.

17. I will refrain from usurping the group and encourage the group members to do the same.

18. I will remind myself that children need to be heard and that they very often "act out" because no one is willing to listen.

19. I will refer any serious personal problems of group members to more experienced personnel rather than try to handle them on my own.

20. I will be as relaxed and as genuinely enthusiastic as possible and enjoy myself with "my little buddies."

Reader Reflections

Insights: _____

_____

_____

_____

_____

Actions for Our School (District) to Consider: _____

_____

_____

_____

_____

_____

_____

_____

*...anytime children can solve their own problems with peers
and reach mutual agreement,
it is growth for all parties involved.*

HAVING A GREAT DAY AT CHICKASHA

These management strategies have led to happy students, teachers, and parents at Chickasha Intermediate School in Oklahoma.

5 The hardest part of teaching school is, undeniably, classroom management. We should know. As three classroom teachers and a principal at Chickasha Intermediate School in Chickasha, Oklahoma, we deal on a daily basis with situations requiring discipline.

Currently, our school has 479 sixth and seventh graders. Jana Dabney teaches sixth and seventh grade reading. Sharon Wilson teaches sixth and seventh grade math and serves one period each day in our ISS/SCC class (In-School-Suspension/Self-Contained Classroom). Rita Cavin teaches seventh grade geography and English. Vickie Holloway is the principal.

Five years ago, when Sharon and Vickie first arrived at Chickasha Intermediate, we were a school with severe discipline problems and plunging morale. As Jana reflects,

JANA DABNEY
Sixth and Seventh Grade Reading

SHARON WILSON
Sixth and Seventh Grade Math

RITA CAVIN
Seventh Grade Geography and English

VICKIE HOLLOWAY
Principal

Chickasha Intermediate School
Chickasha, Oklahoma

"What concerned me most at the time, was not the 380 students acting out, but the 30 adults who stood by and let it happen." In many cases, teachers had become afraid of the students; in other cases, they felt overwhelmed by the number of problems and began to let things slide.

Many parents were concerned about the situation. Some have mentioned since that they considered home schooling as an alternative to sending their child to Intermediate.

Things have changed in the last five years,

however. Not long after Vickie and Sharon came to Intermediate, our staff decided that in order to succeed, we had to come together as a team. It took a lot of patience, planning, and hard work, but today, we are a school that operates on two key words: *pride* and *respect*.

This is the story of how our staff developed both schoolwide and individual classroom management initiatives that turned our

phere and on rewarding positive behavior in order to ensure an appropriate working environment for our students and ourselves.

Schoolwide Initiatives

Our first experience as a team was to meet and design a set of strategies to control student behavior. As we worked together, our mission evolved— Success for All, Now and Tomorrow.

This is the story of how our staff developed both schoolwide and individual classroom management initiatives that turned our school around.

school around. It is also the story of how we continue to work daily on providing a nurturing atmos-

Early Morning Structure

We decided that our first priority was to get students

ready to learn each morning. The morning playground had been chaotic with fights and with students running wild, not paying attention to the directives of the playground supervisor, and generally coming into the school too wired to effectively participate in classroom activities.

The dean of students suggested that we place all students in a structured environment each morning. We decided that as students came to school in the morning, they would take a seat in our rarely used auditorium where they could do homework or read. We also decided that the principal, dean of students, and counselor would greet every student each morning as he or she came into the auditorium. They would send students who were upset, or who

for some other reason were not ready to learn, to talk with one of the staff immediately.

This has proved to be effective, and we have increased its effectiveness by having students sit in homeroom groups and by conducting two DEAR (Drop Everything and Read) sessions a week during this time.

Prior to dismissal from the auditorium each morning, students are instructed to sit up straight and pay attention to the speaker. At this time, a staff member goes over any upcoming events or school problems. (People who come to our assemblies are always in awe of our students' behavior during assemblies.)

Homogeneous Grouping

Our next project was to examine the effectiveness of our developmental

classes, which tended to be a breeding ground for discipline problems. Two teachers agreed not to level their classes for all subjects except math, and to use only high/low grouping there. At the end of the year, they found teaching without the developmental classes to be much easier on classroom management and more academically successful for students in general. Their testimony convinced the other teachers to discontinue developmental classes.

Reward Systems

Around December of that first year, we also decided to reward children for being just plain ole good kids. Vickie contacted one of our industrious parents who organized volunteers to bring ice cream and toppings to school. This was our first attempt to recognize good behavior.

Our Parent-Teachers Organization now conducts a "Positive Incentive Program" every semester in which students who meet the behavioral criteria are rewarded with a party. Here are the criteria: (1) students must have less than three tardies per nine weeks, (2) their record must not show an office referral because of severe behavior problems, and (3) they may not receive more than three teacher-assigned detentions. Last semester, 356 out of 444 students attended the party.

In one of our trying times, we started the "Three Strikes and You're Out" project. Here's how that works: Approximately three weeks before a special event, we announce to the students that the plan is beginning. Each hour, teachers keep track of students who exhibit improper behavior. At the end of the day, the office randomly calls for the strikes given during certain hours (i.e., "Send down the names of persons receiving strikes in second, fifth, and sixth periods."). Each person listed receives one strike. If a student receives three strikes before the day of the special event, he or she may not attend. Along the way, we have adopted a few exceptions to the three-strikes process such as: "A student cannot strike out during one hour," and "A substitute's strikes are not counted." (The students do not know this one!)

Parent Shadowing

One of our teachers shared the idea of parent shadowing with us. In this activity, the parent of a disruptive

child comes to school and follows the child through the school day. This has proved to be very effective. Rarely have we had to use this technique more than once with a student! (Principal shadowing works well, too.)

Self-Contained Classroom

Time and time again, it came to us that we have many, many good students. It's just that a group you can count on both hands makes it seem like behavior is out of control.

For these students, we

initiated a Self-Contained Classroom (SCC) in which they receive personalized instruction in core academic classes. We also teach these students basic social skills such as how to play a game without cheating or fighting.

The room for SCC has a sink and rest room facilities. Students with good behavior who are in SCC are allowed to go out into the hall between classes

...the beginning of the year is extremely important to successful classroom management.

to use the rest room and cafeteria and to go to electives. If their behavior has not been appropriate, the

class becomes completely self-contained, and they are required to use the rest room facilities within the classroom. Even lunch is brought in to them. As students' behavior and attitude improve, they are placed back, one or two courses at a time, into a regular classroom setup.

We developed a multi-criteria instrument to determine who needed to be in this program. Out of 11 students in the program last year, some were eventually referred to day treatment programs, but we also had three stars. These stars made the program worth it. One former SCC student even became a National Junior Honor Society member.

Individual Initiatives

Teachers at Chickasha Intermediate have developed

a number of discipline strategies independent of one another as well. Following are first-person reports from Jana, Sharon, and Rita on some of their personal classroom management techniques.

Jana Dabney's Classroom Initiatives

It has always intrigued me that discipline is what we classroom teachers are professionally judged and evaluated by, yet it is something we receive very little professional training in. For the most part, we receive our lessons in this area from the "School of Hard Knocks" and/or "Experience U."

One thing I have learned from this personal experience is that the beginning of the year is extremely important to successful classroom management. This is when you estab-

lish your particular style of organization. How you handle this time can determine how the rest of the year goes. Some concepts associated with implementing effective classroom management are
• establishing workable rules and procedures,
• giving adequate explanations for rules and procedures, and
• establishing your role as the classroom leader.

Rules to Work By
When I started my first job as a junior high math teacher (my sixth year of teaching experience), one of my new colleagues, in an attempt to show me the ropes, shared a list of official classroom rules that I was to use in my room. There were so many rules, it took all of one side of the paper and half of the other just to list them! I

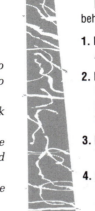

...was really sick. It seemed ...had been hired more as a ...detective/police officer ...han as the math teacher. ...After several attempts to ...absorb this highly com-...plex document, I finally ...sat down and wrote a suc-...cinct list of behaviors that ...I simply couldn't tolerate ...in my classroom. From ...that evolved my own ...rules to work by. To this ...day, I review them with ...all of my students when ...they first enter my class-...room. I then post the list ...in a prominent place for ...the remainder of the year.

Mrs. Dabney's Class-...room Rules

• *If Mrs. Dabney is talk-ing, DON'T!*

• *If assigned, do it (on time, with a smile)!*

• *If you don't want to do it over, do it right the first time!*

• *If it's a school rule, follow it!*

• *If you are supposed to have it, be sure you do EVERY DAY!*

• *If allowed time to work in class, use it wisely!*

• *If you gripe about the assignment, be prepared to do extra!*

• *If you are angry, bite the bullet!*

Following is how I ex-plain these rules to my students:

• *If Mrs. Dabney is talk-ing, DON'T!*

Unfortunately, I talk a lot, so don't even plan on much talking at all!

• *If assigned, do it (on time and with a smile)!*

Keep up with due dates! When you've gone through all the work and are ready to hand it in, do it with a good attitude so I'll think you've put your best work into it. Not: "Here's this stupid paper you wanted." That makes me feel as if you didn't do much work

on it—as if you don't value it.

• *If you don't want to do it over, do it right the first time!*

Pay attention to the rubric on the assignment! Check your work over be-fore you hand it in. I don't like to be the bearer of bad news!

• *If it's a school rule, follow it!*

If the handbook says, "No gum at school," don't ask me if you can chew gum. I follow rules.

• *If you are supposed to have it, be sure you do, every day!*

Would you pay a car-penter who didn't bring his or her tools every day? A doctor? A mechanic? Get in the habit, it's a good one.

• *If allowed time to work, use it wisely!*

If we have some extra time, I will be willing to let you work, not talk.

• *If you gripe about the assignment, be prepared to do extra.*

In Search of Effective Discipline

If you are interested in designing a set of strategies to control student behavior in your school, we suggest you take the following steps.

1. **Develop a site team.**
   A few heads are better than one.

2. **Be creative.**
   Incorporate into your plan those problem-solving strategies you teach your students to use.

3. **Be flexible.**
   Try it; you might like it!

4. **Communicate with colleagues.**
   Realize we all have different ar-eas of strength. Use them.

5. **Read for management ideas.**
   Read everything: education journals, women's magazines, even *Popular Science!*

6. **Keep parents involved.**
   They are eager to be on the team.

7. **Share your successes.**
   You'll soon enjoy hearing about them from the community!

8. **Most of all, love the kids!**

I have carefully planned the work and activities we do in class. If I ask for a two-page paper that describes the setting and main characters in a book we've read, I don't want to hear, "Golly, two pages. Do we *have* to write two pages? What if we...." It's not "Let's Make a Deal"

really make you upset. Come to me before class, just let me know that you are upset, and I'll try to keep things safe for you. But, if someone looks at you, says, "Hi," or smiles at someone else in the classroom, don't bite their head off and start WW III in my room!

not a factor here, only grooming.)

If you look like you are ready to pick weeds or rake leaves, you'll probably have better luck doing that than teaching a classroom full of energized students. Jeans, sweat pants, sloppy-looking clothes make you look "at ease." Students interpret those vibes as "Sic 'em! They're ready to play!"

A high school teacher I know wears suits to school the first week—a jacket, scarf or tie, and skirt. During the second week, she leaves the suit jacket off as long as she has control in the classroom. If the students start getting loud, on goes the jacket. As the students practice good behavior, they learn that she will remain in charge.

Look important; feel important.

Sharon Wilson's Classroom Initiatives

I started teaching when my own kids were in high school, which I feel gives me a degree of insight into student behavior. My first year at Intermediate was basically noneventful except for my seventh grade developmental reading class, which was the last hour of the day.

Have you ever noticed that developmental students also have an inability to stay on task and will misbehave to keep someone from noticing that they are experiencing academic problems? Well, you can imagine trying to teach 20 students like this all together at the end of the day! Do you hear the theme "Mission Impossible" playing?

I have found that the following techniques can help such students under-

...many management problems can be avoided by providing two things: (1) clear guidelines for behavior and work procedures and (2) engaging instruction.

here. I'll just say, "Gee, I think you can write three or four pages on yours."

• *If you are angry, bite the bullet!*

Sometimes something happens in another class or between classes that can

Standards to Dress By

In order to help with discipline, my advice to a first-year teacher is to look professional. Look like you are dressed for an important job. (Interestingly enough, I find that age is tand the importance of rules and develop independence and self-discipline.

Mastery Learning

In October, Vickie came to our faculty meeting and shared information about requiring students to demonstrate mastery. Many teachers didn't think this would work, but I didn't question it. I was willing to try anything to get students to stay on task and out of trouble.

At the time, I was using a newspaper as my primary resource with my developmental students. In keeping with the mastery concept, I decided to check off each daily newspaper assignment, assess it according to pre-established outcomes, and require 85 percent mastery. The amount of time my developmental students spent on task increased dramatically!

Self-Monitoring Forms

Another component that I use from time to time is a self-monitoring form on which the students can monitor their own conduct by focusing on a specific behavior that needs improving, such as talking without permission. We would do this daily, keep it on file, and from time to time, I would assess the results individually with students.

Color-Coded Cards

After Jana shared the classroom rules with the other teachers, Vickie helped me establish a color-coded card system to be used with the rules. I wrote each rule on a poster board in a different color. I then put that corresponding color on an index-card. Now, if after one verbal warning, a student breaks a rule, I simply lay

a card on his or her desk. The student signs, dates, and hands the card back to me. I keep the cards filed by class in a file box on my desk. When a student collects three of any color, I assign detention.

This has proved to be a great success, and instruction time is not interrupted by "What did I do?" The student knows the exact rule he or she has broken by looking at the color on the displayed chart. I might add that rarely are students "surprised" when I assign detention. After all, they have received clear warnings. The card method also enables me to nip problems in the bud. With this system, behavior problems are handled before they reach the out-of-control state.

Traffic-Control Cards

When students appear to

need a more structured environment in which to perform independent tasks (in other words, a way to regulate classroom traffic), I use a self-checking index-card strategy.

First, I place index cards numbered in order from one through 10 inside library-book pockets attached to the wall by the entry door. If a student wants to help correct papers or complete a special learning activity at our learning table, he or she takes the next available card. After class instruction, whomever has cards one through three will go to complete their independent task. Whenever a card is returned to its pocket, the student with the next number goes to the table.

Rita Cavin's Classroom Initiatives

I have come to realize that

many management problems can be avoided by providing two things: (1) clear guidelines for behavior and work procedures and (2) engaging instruction.

Clear Guidelines

I'm not sure why this obvious fact escaped me for such a long time. But as a school teacher, I made

As my colleagues and I examined these assumptions, we realized that students and staff desperately needed a common culture that established the criteria for work and behavior. We learned never to take standards for granted. Before we ask students for anything now, we make our guidelines clear to everyone involved.

behavior problems. We found that Johnson and Johnson's book *Circles of Learning*, was a valuable guide. Several of our faculty spent time reading professional literature on the subject and passing new information on to the rest of the staff. As many have before us, we compiled an impressive array of techniques for structuring classes for cooperative learning.

However, I would often try what seemed like a well-organized and prepared lesson only to hit major snags. It seemed that my students were not as well trained in cooperative learning as I'd assumed they were. That was discouraging. It meant backtracking and re-planning and re-doing. For many teachers around me, it meant they had an excuse for abandoning cooperative

learning altogether and doing what they'd always done.

Because I teach social studies and geography, I felt compelled to keep searching for ways to get my students to cooperate with one another. It just seemed to be the democratic thing to do. And it seemed like a motivating way to learn. After more reading and support from our principal, we discovered that the key to successful cooperative groups lies totally in the groundwork. (That brings me back to my first point about the need to provide students with clear expectations and work guidelines.)

We began to teach the students the general process involved in cooperative learning. This is often called *group process* and fundamentally means that all the general rules,

> *We realized that students and staff desperately needed a common culture that established the criteria for work and behavior.*

many assumptions about students' behavior and work habits. I assumed they knew what was expected of them and that they knew the processes they needed to follow to meet those expectations.

Engaging Instruction

In reading about effective practice in middle schools, staff members found many references to cooperative learning—how it actively engaged learners and seemed to minimize easons, purposes, and procedures of group work are dealt with before any assignments are made. We found that the first two weeks of each new school year were an excellent time for teaching process. During that time, each teacher in a team would teach a different segment of the process. This way, all the students were involved in all the aspects of process without having to hear it six or seven times. After establishing the guidelines and signal words or cues, each teacher in a team would have all students familiar with all the necessary background.

We found that having common rules and cues in our team simplifies life for everyone involved. Because our sixth graders come from self-contained classrooms, usually with a single teacher, into our teams of five core teachers, unifying the team helps both students and parents with the adjustment.

One special part of the general group process we teach our students is a technique for listening. In 1991, our school counselor arranged for a special assembly from Motivational Media Assemblies, Inc., of Burbank, California. As part of the program, the presenters furnished students with materials to help them develop interpersonal skills. In these materials, we discovered and adopted as our school's own, a listening technique called OLE (we pronounce it *oh-lay*). Students are taught three steps to effective listening:

1. Open posture; uncross legs and arms.
2. Lean forward.
3. Make eye contact.

This has proved to be effective in the classroom and in larger groups of students in helping students to focus their attention.

Looking back, it seems more than obvious that we all do better when we know what is expected of us. This applies to adults and students alike. My job as the "teacher" is to equip each student with tools they can use to build their own learning. Teaching process helps me do that job.

Conclusion

"We are having a great day at Chickasha Intermediate" is the slogan we use when we answer the telephone at school these days, and this is totally appropriate. It reflects the school that Intermediate has become.

We have happy kids and parents. Student attendance is up, and when we have student-led parent conferences at the end of the first and third nine weeks, 97% of parents attend. During open house, our auditorium is standing room only.

We've come a long way from the days when large numbers of students acted out, when many staff members withdrew, and when many parents fretted.

...today, we are a school that operates on two key words: pride and respect.

Today, we are a team that is meeting its mission—Success for All, Now and Tomorrow.◆

The OLE Listening Technique

1 Open posture; uncross legs and arms.

2 Lean forward.

3 Make eye contact.

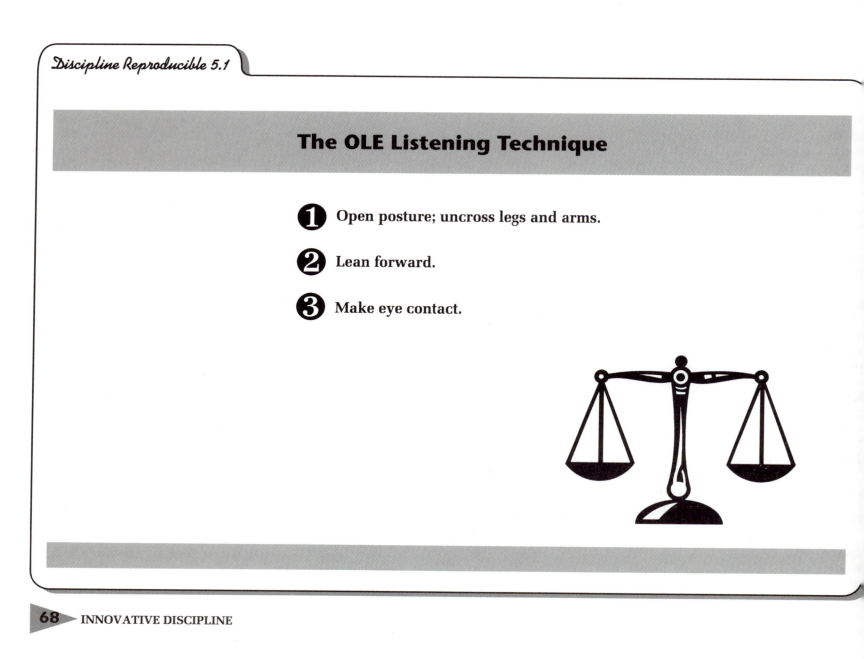

Before You Implement Cooperative Learning

The following guidelines can help minimize any problems that might occur when you introduce cooperative learning procedures.

1. **Start slowly.**
   Use cooperative learning sparingly until you are sure that what you are doing is benefiting your class.

2. **Avoid group grading.**
   Group grading can alarm parents of high achievers. Group grading is only for skilled practitioners of cooperative learning, and then only when adequate parent and administrator information has been provided in advance.

3. **Build an atmosphere that encourages cooperative learning.**
   Building student ownership, active participation, high expectations, and positive feelings creates a foundation for cooperative learning and for successful classroom management.

4. **Promote student success.**
   Early experiences with cooperative learning should be highly successful and rewarding for students.

5. **Tell administrators you are using cooperative learning methods.**
   Be ready to explain your goals, expected outcomes, and the benefits research associates with cooperative learning.

Before You Implement Cooperative Learning
(Continued)

6. Use other techniques and strategies as well as cooperative learning.
No technique is effective when used all the time.

7. Monitor student reactions and conduct individual conferences with students.
This helps reassure those who are troubled by cooperative learning.

8. Teach group process to students.
Don't expect your students to already have the skills needed to work successfully in groups.

9. Monitor the effectiveness of your teaching.
Use the same individual evaluation procedures you usually use. You may also wish to monitor student achievement; attitude; attendance; discipline referrals; and behavior in the playground, hallway, and lunchroom as indicators of the success of your methods.

10. Network with other teachers.
A support group of other teachers who use cooperative learning is necessary for problem solving, celebration, and exchange of ideas.

SOURCE: *Cooperative Learning in the Elementary Classroom*, by Lawrence Lyman, Harvey C. Foyle, and Tara S. Azwell. Washington, D. C.: National Education Association, 1993.

Insights: _____

_____

_____

_____

_____

Actions for Our School (District) to Consider: _____

_____

_____

_____

_____

_____

_____

_____

MANAGING YOUR OWN FLIGHT PLAN

High School students learn the value of self-directed behavior at this dropout recovery school in California.

6 Although I have been a classroom teacher for more than 20 years, and all of those years have been stimulating and rewarding, what I am doing right now is the most exciting job I have had. It is also, by far, the most challenging. I am the coordinator/ teacher of the Independent Learning Center (ILC), a dropout recovery school in the Woodland Joint Unified School District in Woodland, California.

Basically, I am working with all of the students that no one else wants to deal with: the habitual truants, the incorrigibles, the drug/alcohol addicted, the violent, and the lost. Sometimes people ask what I did wrong and whom I offended to be "put" into such an environment.

Let me set your mind at ease. No one "put" me here. This school did not exist in our district before I designed it, brought it to life, and began teaching here. The ILC is an independent-study program that came into existence by way of a grant I wrote along with Carol Murphy and Pat Blevins Turner, two elementary teaching colleagues in my district. The grant was designed to study at-risk students and to support them in becoming more successful

SANDI REDENBACH
Coordinator/Teacher
The Independent Learning Center
Woodland, California

in school. At the time, the program was just that, a program, not a school. When the grant money, given by the National Foundation for the Improvement of Education (NFIE), ran out, our superintendent, Robert Watt, came to me and asked how I might institutionalize the program. After I shared with him what I envisioned—a high school for providing at-risk students an opportunity to choose success through a philosophy that promotes integrated discipline, individual responsibility, and self-esteem—somewhat hesitantly, he said, "Let's do it as a pilot program." Creating the school could not have happened without the blessing, encouragement, and support of such a trusting and empowering educator!

Today, we are more than six years strong and enroll approximately 60 students. The school is a large, open space. Students do much of their work independently, but they attend many student-teacher conferences that provide important guidance and instructional interaction.

The following is the story of the ILC's conception, its first six years of life, and how it continues to develop successful, self-directed individuals.

Integrated Discipline

You could say that the first ideas for the school started more than 17 years ago. After my third year in the Woodland district, I began to notice that some students were having extreme behavior problems in certain teachers' classes. Those same students, however, were not having difficulties in other teachers' classes.

I began to talk with these kids about what seemed to be the problems in certain classes. During the next few years, I watched for and documented repeated occurrences, both with the teachers and the students. And what I discovered was that those teachers who managed discipline outside of the curriculum —in other words, those teachers who had just a list of rules and regulations for getting along in the classroom, and said what the consequences for not following those rules would be, and expected the students to follow them without question— documentably had more problems than those teachers who managed discipline by integrating the "rules" and expectations into the daily learning environment.

How Does Integration Work?

By observing the successful teachers, I learned that the first step toward integrating discipline into the learning environment/curriculum is to establish rules for the classroom— but just two or three. Today, my three are as follows:

1. There will be no putdowns, insults, or unkind language used toward the teacher, your peers, or yourself.

2. You will come prepared to learn, with books, paper, pens, homework, and with an open mind, healthy body, and positive attitude.

3. We will do all that it takes to create and support a safe space in which all

> *...those teachers who managed discipline outside of the curriculum...had more problems than those who managed discipline by integrating the "rules" and expectations into the daily learning environment.*

nay learn.

I invite students to generate any other "rules" that they believe they might need in order to enforce the other three. Generally speaking, they do not feel that other rules are necessary. Neither do I. If students embraced those three all the time it would be a wonderful, peaceful environment, perhaps even a bit boring.

Because we can always count on students to be human, they will "test" the rules. This is where integrated discipline comes in to play. We must begin the teaching process out of the so-called misbehaviors of others. We can turn each one into a "teachable" moment.

Whatever we have to teach regarding a misbehavior can be addressed through the classroom rules. It is not difficult to

begin to see how almost all behavior fits either positively or negatively into them. As teachers do this, they should adhere to the following guidelines:

1. Do not judge students' behavior. Simply assist them in getting back on track toward being responsible once again.

2. Help students accept the natural consequences of their behavior (i.e., apologizing for causing hurt feelings or inconvenience, restructuring a previous agreement, losing a time-sensitive opportunity). Next time, they can choose to act in a more responsible manner.

3. Assist students to process what caused them to act irresponsibly so they can avoid acting that way in the future.

Our students learn quickly that self-directed

behavior is about being willing to accept the consequences and/ or the outcomes for both the positive and negative choices one makes.

Modeling

Modeling is another effective way to integrate discipline instruction into the learning environment. For example, students internalize what we classroom teachers value from the mood and tone we set. They see how we work in a collegial fashion and listen as we respectfully exchange information. They know that the gentle and honest communication we use produces a consequence that the students would enjoy in their own interactions. And they realize quickly from this behavior that some things are not negotiable, such as respecting another's rights.

Our School District

Woodland Joint Unified School District is located outside Sacramento, California, in a fairly rural community. The school district has 12 elementary schools, two junior high schools (grades seven through nine), one comprehensive traditional high school (grades 10 through 12), a continuation high school, and our school, the Independent Learning Center. The ethnic breakdown of the student body is approximately 55 percent Anglo, 40 percent Hispanic, and five percent Asian. Occasionally, we have an African-American student. Our high school dropout rate is approximately 35 percent.

Woodland, California, is a relatively small town whose main sources of entertainment come from its high schools, mostly in the form of sporting events and plays. It is a town with many families of solid citizen background, some of whom take pride in the schools. The truth is that our district is not much different from the majority of rural school districts throughout the United States, except that we have a few fairly wealthy farmers (rice and tomatoes are the leading cash crops).

Self-Responsibility

Students need to be made aware that they actually choose their behavior, and as a result, choose the consequences of their behavior and choose how others relate to them.

For example, when students come to us at the ILC, they often talk about how mean teachers have been to them in the past, how they were always picked on, how they were forced to do certain things, and so on. When this "I Am the Victim of Evil Teachers" topic comes up, I direct a series of questions to the accusing students. The questions are

of such a conversation might be something like:

I ask: "Why do you suppose all of those teachers chose to treat you so differently than they treated the other students?"

They answer: "They just didn't like me."

My next question is: "How could that be possible when you are obviously a wonderful, charming human being?"

My response is usually: "So now that you realize that when you exhibit that quality of behavior, you create that quality of relationship, what do you suppose you could do to take charge of changing your relationships with teachers?"

Answers to that question vary, but most students begin to understand in just an instant, without blame or anger, who is really responsible for the consequences of their behavior.

your own plane, and worse yet, you don't know who is in the cockpit. When that is the case, it is even possible that the plane has been hijacked. If a person does not want that to be the story of his life—letting someone else be the pilot and ending up wherever that pilot wants to land—then it is necessary to take charge of the flight plan, the condition of the plane you are flying in, and the actual piloting of the plane.

Students need to be made aware that they actually choose their behavior, and as a result, choose the consequences of their behavior and choose how others relate to them.

designed to allow and encourage self-discipline; the answers the students generate are often more revealing to them than to their teachers. A sample

Their answer is most likely some sort of acknowledgment about the less-than-cooperative behavior they may have exhibited.

Personal Goal Setting

At the ILC, we explain to students that if they are responsible for their behavior, then they must set personal goals for themselves. We use the following analogy to demonstrate why.

If life is an airplane, and you don't file a flight plan, you are not piloting

Some psychologists and education researchers believe that setting personal goals (to complete a project, hone a skill, solve a problem, obtain the necessary training required of a specific career) has the most immediate motivational effect on a person's behavior. According to researcher M. M. Clifford, such goals can serve at

east five functions:

1. to guide and direct behavior

2. to focus attention and effort in a given direction

3. to serve as a standard or ideal for measuring progress

4. to lead to a restructuring of activities and procedures that increase efficiency

5. to reflect values and motives of the individual.

In helping students set goals, you may find the following suggestions useful.

1. Help reluctant goal setters to concentrate on a single goal for a short period of time so that they can measure their progress and maintain interest.

2. Encourage students to state their goals clearly so that they know exactly what must be done to meet the goals.

3. Although the teacher may suggest possible objectives, students should select what they choose to work toward, and within what framework.

4. Encourage students to change or adjust goals as their needs and perceptions change.

5. Help students to set short-term as well as long-term goals. While reaching short-term goals is important, students should be made to understand that developing self-directedness and prosocial behavior are long-term procedures. They can aspire to them through a series of short-term goals.

Developing Work Contracts

At the ILC, we also develop work contracts with our students. This takes time, assistance, understanding, and patience on the part of teachers, but our teachers realize that if students are going to succeed, they must be clear about what behaviors we expect from students in specific learning situations.

We work with our students—no matter where they are in the process of living responsible, disciplined, self-actualized lives—to develop a two-page contract for each independent-study course they take. The contract covers instructional objectives and methods of evaluating these objectives as well as a list of homework assignments that equals a minimum of 30 hours of out-of-class work per course. (See Discipline Reproducibles 6.3a and 6.3b for an example of a two-page contract.)

We find that these contracts help students affirm that even though they have lots of challenges in their lives, their first re-

sponsibility is to their schoolwork.

Self-Esteem

Regardless of the condition of a student's self-concept upon entering school, teachers do have the potential to help boost a student's sense of self-esteem, which in turn, can go a long way toward encouraging positive self-directed behavior. According to researchers M. Kash and G. Borich, teachers can help students develop self-esteem through the following actions.

1. Recognize and affirm the value of each student.

2. Keep in mind that the fundamental basis for acquiring self-esteem in the classroom is the student's reflection of self as an achiever.

3. Help students learn to value the assessment of their performance and products by establishing a clear, positive relationship between evaluative processes and achievement.

> *At the ILC, we explain to students that if they are responsible for their behavior, then they must set personal goals for themselves.*

4. Clearly model the proper use of self-criticism and self-reward.

5. Accurately communicate and interpret the standards used for evaluating performances and products in the classroom.

6. Help students acquire and allow them to use evaluative skills.

7. Make the individual student improvement the value underlying competitive activity in the classroom.

8. Associate teacher praise and criticism with specific elements of student performance, reinforcing positive aspects and providing a basis for improving negative aspects of student work.

Conclusion

Some days my colleagues and I slip back into the old ways of just letting an action go by, but we soon reflect on how we can really use potentially negative discipline problems as teachable moments, and we realize the value of making that habit stick. We see, by the extraordinary strides our students make, just how effective this process is in motivating behavior.

Our students tell us in the exit essays they write that the thing they learned the most was how to take responsibility for their own behavior management and that before coming to the ILC they felt "out of control."

To quote one of our students, one who, incidentally, had been absent more than 54 days during her last attempt at "regular" school: "It's a good school for certain types of kids because it gives us a chance to work for ourselves and still have help. In regular school you have to do what you are told when you are told. I was never good at that. At the ILC, I am getting it done on my own. It makes me feel capable."

Now that Superintendent Watt has retired, we expect some changes. But we will face the challenge of change, as we continue enjoying the sense of accomplishment we have felt in the past.

At the ILC, we will continue to teach the hard to reach. We will continue to reach the hard to teach, because every human being deserves to be a self-directed, empowered, contributing, human being.◆

Goal-Setting Sequence

In his famous "Pawns to Origins" study, education researcher R. de Charms used this goal-setting sequence to help elementary students learn to act successfully:

1. Analyze personal strengths and weaknesses.

2. Choose personal goals realistically, noting individual capabilities and realities of the situation.

3. Select immediate, concrete actions that can be taken now.

4. Determine ways to tell whether action is goal-oriented.

What About Teacher Behavior?

There are several teacher behaviors we can practice that can help students truly "choose" success.

1. We can learn about and understand the ways in which self-esteem is developed and nourished and decide to incorporate that knowledge into our teaching.

2. We can relate to all students as though they are our clients and as though our living depended upon them and the way we serve them.

3. We can familiarize ourselves with learning/personality styles and engage all students in assignments that match the style in which they learn best.

4. We can model empowering and enhancing communication patterns in order for students to access them in their own lives.

5. We can acknowledge that self-discipline is difficult for ourselves as well as students and that it takes lots of opportunities to practice until we get it right.

6. We can commit to using active listening skills, lots of humor, and to never using sarcasm.

Woodland Joint Unified School District
Independent Learning Center

Independent Study Contract

Course No. 301   **Date** _____

Course Title _Literature-Composition C_

Student Name _____ Phones (H) _____

GO # _____ Birth Date _____ Age _____ (W) _____

Supervising Teacher _Sandi Redenbach_

Instructor/Student Meetings: Day _____ Time _____ Place _ILC_

Student Objectives:

In this course, students will read and write about American short stories and modern American nonfiction. Students will write paragraphs and compositions about the literature. Students will also select a novel, read it, and write about it. Students must pass all tests with a score of 70% or higher.

Methods of Evaluating Objectives: 1. _Student/teacher discussions_
                                          2. _Written work_
                                          3. _Tests: objective, essay, oral_

Units Attempted _____ Duration of Contract: Beginning Date _____ Ending Date _____

Agreement:

One unit of high school credit will be granted for fifteen (15) productive hours of academic work. One unit of high school credit will be granted for twelve (12) hours of productive activity if this is a physical education contract.

This contract may be terminated if the student: (a) consistently fails to complete weekly assignments or (b) misses three instructor/student meetings without an attempt to make up the time or assignments.

We have read the above contract and agree to the conditions as stated.

Student's Signature _____ Date _____ Supervising Teacher's Signature _____ Date _____

Parent/Guardian's Signature _____ Date _____ Other Assisting Person's Signature _____ Date _____

Certification:

Units Attempted _____ Grade _____

Units Granted _____ Date Credit Recorded _____

Supervising Teacher's Signature _____ Registrar's Initials _____

Independent Study Contract
(page two)

Course Title and Number _Literature-Composition C #301_

Text _American Literature—McDougal Littell & Co._

Assignments:

1. Read the unit introduction.
2. Read everything in each unit, including works and bibliographical information.
3. Answer in complete sentences all questions at the end of each work.
4. Work through textbook pages 947-976. Section is entitled "Handbook: How to Write About Literature." Complete all assignments highlighted in blue.
5. In addition, select one novel from the attached list, read it, and write an essay on a topic you determine with the teacher.

Progress:

Pages	Assignments Accepted	Tests Passed (Score)
386-470		
471-563		
564-602		
603-637		

Novel Selected _____

Essay Completed _____

Oral and/or Written Exam _____

Sample Exit Essay

I first learned of the Independent Learning Center (ILC) while attending school at the Teen Parent Center. I was in my senior year and needed more credits than I could earn there. So I took some extra classes at the ILC at the same time. I was enrolled at the Independent Learning Center for a little over a year, and then I graduated.

Some classes I really enjoyed taking were "Working Today and Tomorrow" and "Foods." These courses helped me realize what direction I wanted to go in when I moved on to achieve a higher level of education. My favorite course at the ILC was "Personal Development." This was a very interesting and time-consuming course that made me do a lot of thinking about myself and the way I act. I honestly believe that I finished that course a better person. My self-esteem is much higher because I look at myself differently. I am able to think before I act, look at both sides of a situation, and stay calm. I feel really good because of this.

I enjoyed going to school at the Independent Learning Center because it challenged me to teach myself the courses I took. At a traditional school, I wouldn't have had that chance.

(Continued on next page.)

Sample Exit Essay
(Continued)

The teachers at this school are really wonderful people. The first one I met was Sandi, and I liked her instantly. While there were times that she scared me a little, there were also times that she made me feel good about myself by telling me how smart I was. Then I met Amy, who was a substitute at the ILC. She was really nice to me, and I don't believe I've ever seen her without a smile on her face. Next, I met Carol. She was very easy to talk to and was very understanding with me. When I started attending the Independent Learning Center full time, I met Lance. I enjoyed talking to him, and I think he is a great teacher who is very smart. Then there was Vicki. She is the secretary at ILC. I felt that she was a very nice person, and she was always cheerful. This school is full of terrific, encouraging teachers, and I think they're all wonderful people.

I would like to talk about my future plans now. I have decided to attend a culinary academy and then take some business and nutrition courses at Sacramento City College. This way I will be qualified for anything from catering to restaurant management. I am very interested in foods and cooking, and I feel like this would be a very rewarding field to get into.

I want to thank everyone at the Independent Learning Center for being there and being so nice to me.

Layla S.
1-12-93

Reader Reflections

Insights: _____

_____

_____

_____

_____

Actions for Our School (District) to Consider: _____

_____

_____

_____

_____

_____

Selected Resources

Books

Barth, R. 1990. *Improving Schools from Within*. San Francisco: Jossey-Bass.

Benjamin, A. 1978. *Behavior in Small Groups*. Boston: Houghton Mifflin.

Benninga, J. S. 1991. *Moral, Character, and Civic Education in the Elementary School*. New York: Teachers College Press.

Berkowitz, M. W., and Oser, F. eds. 1988. *Moral Education: Theory and Application*. Hillsdale, N.J.: Erlbaum.

Bonstingl, J. J. 1993. *Schools of Quality: An Introduction to Total Quality Management in Education*. Alexandria, Va.: Association for Supervision and Curriculum Development.

Byrnes, M. A., and Cornesky, R. A. 1992. *The Quality Teacher: Implementing Total Quality Management in the Classroom*. Port Orange, Fla: Cornesky and Associates Press.

Canfield, J., and Wells, H. 1976. *100 Ways to Enhance Self-Concept in the Classroom*. Englewood Cliffs, N.J.: Prentice-Hall.

Cangelosi, J. S. 1990. *Cooperation in the Classroom: Students and Teachers Together*. Washington, D.C.: National Education Association.

Canter, L., and Canter, M. 1976. *Assertive Discipline: A Take-Charge Approach for Today's Educator*. Seal Beach, Calif.: Canter and Associates.

Carruthers, B., and Coleman, J. 1987. *Legitimacy and Social Structure: Authority in High Schools*. Chicago: University of Chicago Press.

Casanova, V., Berliner, D. C., and Placier, P. 1990. *Classroom Management*. Readings in Educational Research Series. Washington, D.C.: National Education Association.

Charles, C. M. 1989. *Building Classroom Discipline: From Models to Practice*, 3d edition. White Plains, N.Y.: Longman, Inc.

Chase, L. 1975. *The Other Side of the Report Card*. Ann Arbor, Mich.: Goodrich Publishing.

Clarke, J. 1985. *Who Me Lead a Group?* New York: Winston Press.

Curwin, R. L., and Mendler, A. N. 1988. *Discipline with Dignity*. Alexandria, Va.: Association for Supervision and Curriculum Development.

deCharms, R. 1976. *Enhancing Motivation: Change in the Classroom*. New York: Wiley.

Deming, W. E. 1986. *Out of the Crisis*. Cambridge, Mass.: Massachusetts Institute of Technology, Center for Advanced Engineering Study.

Duke, D. L. ed. 1982. *Helping Teachers Manage Classrooms*. Alexandria, Va.: Association for Supervision and Curriculum Development.

Eldaro, P., and Cooper, M. 1977. *AWARE (Activities for Social Development)*. Reading, Mass.: Addison-Wesley.

Elias, M. J., and Tobias, S. E. 1990. *Problem Solving/ Decision Making for Social and Academic Success*. Washington, D.C.: National Education Association.

Emmer, E. T., Evertson, C. M., Clements, B. S., and Worsham, M. E. 1984. *Classroom Management for Secondary Teachers*. Englewood Cliffs, N.J.: Prentice-Hall.

Evertson, C. M., Emmer, E. T., Clements, B. S., Sanford, J. P., and Worsham, M. E. 1984. *Classroom Management for Elementary Teachers*. Englewood Cliffs, N.J.: Prentice-Hall.

Gabor, A. 1990. *The Man Who Discovered Quality*. New York: Times Books.

Galvin, J. C., and Veerman, D. R. 1991. *Harmony*. Burbank, Calif.: Motivational Media Assemblies.

Glasser, W. 1986. *Control Theory in the Classroom*. New York: Harper and Row.

Glasser, W. 1992. *The Quality School: Managing Students Without Coercion*. New York: HarperPerennial.

Gordon, T. 1989. *Discipline that Works: Promoting Self-Discipline in Children*. New York: Penguin.

Hargreaves, D., and Hopkins, D. 1991. *The Empowered School*. London: Cassell.

Harmin, M. *Inspiring Discipline: A Practical Guide for Today's Schools*. Washington, D.C.: National Education Association. Forthcoming.

Johnson, D. W., Johnson, R. T., and Holubec, E. J. 1984. *Circles of Learning*. Alexandria, Va.: Association for Supervision and Curriculum Development.

Johnson, D. W., and Johnson, R. T. 1991. *Teaching Students to be Peacemakers*. Edina, Minn.: Interaction Books.

Kohut, S., and Range, D. G. 1986. *Classroom Discipline: Case Studies and Viewpoints*, 2d edition. Washington, D.C.: National Education Association.

Kounin, J. 1970. *Discipline and Group Management in Classrooms*. New York: Holt, Rinehart, and Winston.

Kreidler, W. J. 1984. *Creative Conflict Resolution*. Glenview, Ill.: Scott, Foresman.

Lehr, J. B., and Harris, H. W. 1988. *At-Risk, Low-Achieving Students in the Classroom*. Washington, D.C.: National Education Association.

Lyman, L., Foyle, H. F., and Azwell, T. S. 1993. *Cooperative Learning in the Elementary Classroom*. Washington, D.C.: National Education Association.

Maggs, M. M. 1980. *The Classroom Survival Book: A Practical Manual for Teachers*. New York: Franklin Watts.

Nelsen, J. 1981. *Positive Discipline*. New York: Ballantine Books.

Nucci, L. ed. 1989. *Moral Development and Character Education: A Dialogue*. Berkeley, Calif.: McCutchan.

Presbie, R. J., and Brown, P. L. 1985. *Behavior Modification*, 2d edition. Washington, D.C.: National Education Association.

Purkey, W. W., and Stanley, P. H. 1991. *Invitational Teaching, Learning, and Living*. Washington, D.C.: National Education Association.

Raffini, J. P. 1988. *Student Apathy: The Protection of Self-Worth*. Washington, D.C.: National Education Association.

Redenbach, S. 1991. *Self-Esteem: The Necessary Ingredient for Success*. Davis, Calif.: Esteem Seminar Programs and Publications.

Sarason, S. 1971. *The Culture of the School and the Problem of Change*. Newton, Mass.: Allyn & Bacon.

Schell, L. M., and Burden, P. 1992. *Countdown to the First Day of School*. Washington, D.C.: National Education Association.

Schrumpf, F., Crawford, D. K., and Usadel, H. C. 1991. *Peer Mediation: Conflict Resolution in the Schools*. Champaign, Ill.: Research Press.

Schwartz, S., and Pollishuke, M. 1991. *Creating the Child-Centered Classroom*. Canada: Richard C. Owen Publishers.

Senge, P. M. 1990. *The Fifth Discipline: The Art and Practice of the Learning Organization*. New York: Doubleday.

Shewhart, W. A. 1939. *Statistical Method from the Viewpoint of Quality Control*. Washington, D.C.: U.S. Department of Agriculture.

Shuman, R. B. 1989. *Classroom Encounters: Problems, Case Studies, Solutions.* Washington, D.C.: National Education Association.

Silvernail, D. L. 1985. *Developing Positive Student Self-Concept*, 2d edition. Washington, D.C.: National Education Association.

Slavin, R. E. 1981. *Student Team Learning: A Practical Guide to Cooperative Learning*, 3d edition. Washington, D.C.: National Education Association.

Swick, K. J. 1991. *Discipline: Toward Positive Student Behavior.* Washington, D.C.: National Education Association.

Walton, M. 1986. *The Deming Management Method.* New York: Putnam.

Wlodkowski, R. J. 1986. *Motivation.* Washington, D.C.: National Education Association.

Articles
Bonstingl, J. J. 1992. "The Total Quality Classroom." *Educational Leadership* 49(6), 66-70.

Johnson, D. W., Johnson, R. T., Dudley, B., and Burnett, R. 1992. "Teaching Students to be Peer Mediators." *Educational Leadership* 50(1), 10-13.

Rhodes, L. A. 1992. "On the Road to Quality." *Educational Leadership* 49(6), 76-80.

Scherer, M. 1992. "Solving Conflicts: Not Just for Children." *Educational Leadership* 50(1), 14-18.

Willis, S. 1993. "Creating Total Quality Schools." *Educational Leadership* 50(2), 1, 4-5.

Willis, S. 1993. "Helping Students Resolve Conflict: Schools Are Teaching Negotiation, Peer Mediation Skills." *ASCD Update* 35(10), 4-5, 8.

Magazines
Educational Leadership 50(3). This entire issue (November 1992) is devoted to the topic, "Improving School Quality."

Audiotapes
Redenbach, S. 1992. *Self-Esteem: The Necessary Ingredient for Success.* Davis, Calif.: Esteem Seminar Programs and Publications.

Videos

Canter, L., and Canter, M. 1989. *Assertive Discipline for Secondary School Educators*. Inservice video package and leader's manual. Santa Monica, Calif.: Lee Canter and Associates.

Foyle, H. F., and Lyman, L. 1993. *The Interactive Classroom: Cooperative Learning*. Washington, D.C.: National Education Association.

National Education Association, and The Learning Channel. 1993. *Effective Discipline Strategies*. Teacher TV episode 29. Washington, D.C.: NEA Professional Library Video.

National Education Association, and The Learning Channel. 1993. *When Society's Problems Walk through the Door*. Teacher TV episode 23. Washington, D.C.: NEA Professional Library Video.

Schrumpf, F., and Crawford, D. K. 1991. *The Peer Mediation Video: Conflict Resolution in Schools*. Champaign, Ill.: Research Press.

Notes:

_____

_____

_____

_____

_____

_____

Personal Resources

Individuals: _____   _____

_____   _____

_____   _____

_____   _____

_____   _____

_____   _____

_____   _____

Publications: _____   _____

_____   _____

_____   _____

_____   _____

_____ _____

_____ _____

_____ _____

_____

Organizations: _____ _____

_____ _____

_____ _____

_____ _____

_____ _____

_____ _____

_____ _____

_____ _____

Glossary

Assertive Discipline
A disciplinary system based on externally imposed rewards and punishments.

Behavior
The manner of conducting oneself; what one "does."

Behavior Management
A system of rules, sanctions, and rewards that encourage students to exhibit specific behavior and/or accomplish required tasks.

Behavior Modification
Teaching procedure designed to improve behavior.

Classroom Management
Used to be synonymous with *discipline*. The term now includes everything teachers must manipulate in order to produce successful student involvement and cooperation. This includes room arrangement, curriculum, instructional techniques, and classroom rules and expectations.

Conflict Resolution
Teaching students constructive ways to solve conflicts such as training them in ways to mediate and negotiate disputes and developing a school climate that fosters collaborative problem solving.

Developmental Discipline
A discipline system that students themselves participate in creating and monitoring. Emphasizes student understanding of the general principles behind rules, student autonomy, and student input in rule setting and decision making.

Discipline
A process whereby individuals, in interaction with their environment, acquire a behavior syndrome that guides their actions.

Extrinsic Motivation
Emphasizes the value an individual places on the ends of an action. In extrinsic motivation, the goal rather than the doing is the reason for performing the behavior.

Integrated Discipline
A system of discipline that integrates behavior rules and expectations into the daily learning environment.

Intrinsic Motivation
Refers to the pleasure or value associated with an activity itself. In intrinsic motivation, the "doing" is considered the primary reason for the performance of the behavior.

Motivation
Describes those processes that can: (1) arouse and instigate behavior, (b) give direction or purpose to behavior, and (3) lead to choosing or preferring a particular behavior.

Peer Mediation Program
Program in which a group of students are specially trained to help their schoolmates resolve disputes. Peer mediators do not impose solutions; rather, they help the "disputants" work out their own solution to the conflict. Usually, mediators work alone or in pairs.

Prosocial
Promoting individual and group well-being.

Punishment
Any event following a behavior that decreases the occurrence of the behavior in the future.

Quality Time
Classroom time in which all students are engaged in learning something new and meaningful, and doing so in a manner that keeps them interested in and involved with the learning task.

Reinforcement
Any event following a behavior that increases the occurrence of the behavior in the future.

Self-Esteem
Confidence and satisfaction in oneself.

Support Group
A group of persons that provides emotional support and problem-solving advice to one another.

Total Quality Management (TQM)
A process of improving the quality of organizational activities by changing systems rather than changing people.

Discipline is teaching and learning; it is <u>not</u> punishment.

Sylvester Kohut, Jr.
Dale G. Range
Authors of <u>Classroom Discipline:</u>
<u>Case Studies and Viewpoints</u>